# the production manual*

## *a graphic design handbook

An AVA Book
Published by AVA Publishing SA
Rue des Fontenailles 16
Case Postale
1000 Lausanne 6
Switzerland
Tel: +41 786 005 109
Email: enquiries@avabooks.ch

Distributed by Thames & Hudson (ex-North America)
181a High Holborn
London WC1V 7QX
United Kingdom
Tel: +44 20 7845 5000
Fax: +44 20 7845 5055
Email: sales@thameshudson.co.uk
www.thamesandhudson.com

Distributed in the USA & Canada by:
Watson-Guptill Publications
770 Broadway
New York, New York 10003
USA
Fax: +1 646 654 5487
Email: info@watsonguptill.com
www.watsonguptill.com

English Language Support Office
AVA Publishing (UK) Ltd.
Tel: +44 1903 204 455
Email: enquiries@avabooks.co.uk

ISBN 2-940373-63-9 and 978-2-940373-63-5

10 9 8 7 6 5 4 3 2 1

Design and text by Gavin Ambrose and Paul Harris

Production by AVA Book Production Pte. Ltd., Singapore
Tel: +65 6334 8173
Fax: +65 6259 9830
Email: production@avabooks.com.sg

**River Island (above)**
This loose-leaf publication was created for fashion retailer River Island by
Third Eye Design. It features overprinting of red and black inks and a nesting
of different sheets to serve as an informal binding. The folios bleed off the
corners of the sheets, creating a sense of immediacy and anarchy to
the publication.

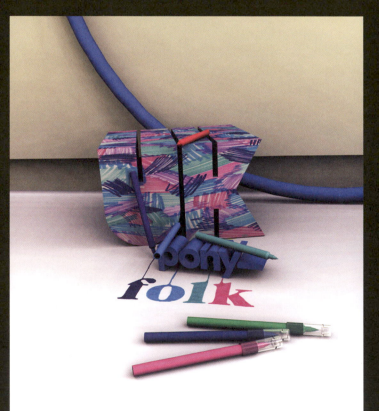

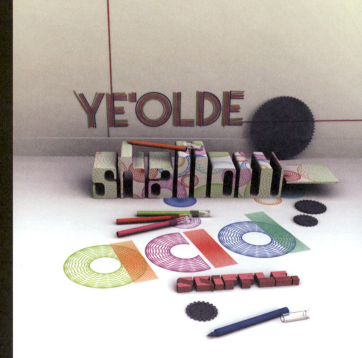

# the production manual*

## *a graphic design handbook

**Ministry of Sound, Saturday Sessions, May–July 2007 (facing page)**
These posters were created for the Ministry of Sound by Studio Output, and aim to reflect the diversity of musical styles catered for by the Saturday Sessions. Based on the epic typography used for the *Ben Hur* film poster, the letters have been playfully reduced to a miniature, transient form and enhanced by the addition of colour from felt-tipped pens.

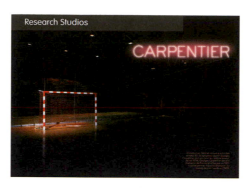

3 Deep Design

Research Studios

Webb & Webb

# how to get the most out of this book

This book offers an in-depth study of the six principle areas of screen and print production. Each chapter provides examples of print-production techniques from leading contemporary design studios, all accompanied by detailed discussions of the reasons behind such design choices from a production perspective.

**colour coding**
Each chapter is colour coded for easy reference.

**navigation bar**
The navigation bar at the top of each section provides at-a-glance information about previous sections and those yet to come, while also allowing for easy cross-referencing.

**chapter introductions**
Each chapter has a clear introduction to establish its purpose.

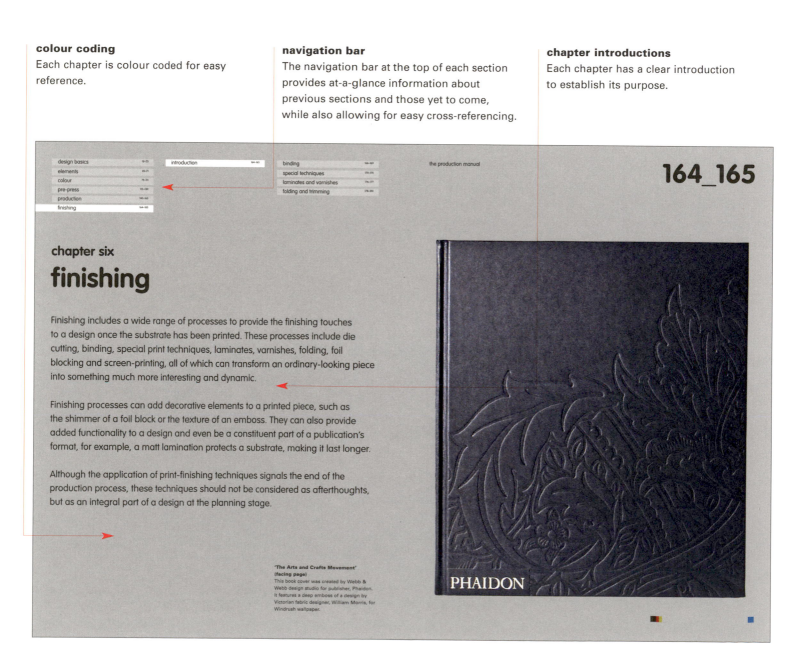

the production manual

**164_165**

chapter six

## finishing

Finishing includes a wide range of processes to provide the finishing touches to a design once the substrate has been printed. These processes include die cutting, binding, special print techniques, laminates, varnishes, folding, foil blocking and screen-printing, all of which can transform an ordinary-looking piece into something much more interesting and dynamic.

Finishing processes can add decorative elements to a printed piece, such as the shimmer of a foil block or the texture of an emboss. They can also provide added functionality to a design and even be a constituent part of a publication's format, for example, a matt lamination protects a substrate, making it last longer.

Although the application of print-finishing techniques signals the end of the production process, these techniques should not be considered as afterthoughts, but as an integral part of a design at the planning stage.

'The Arts and Crafts Movement' (facing page)
This book cover was created by Webb & Webb design studio for publisher, Phaidon. It features a deep emboss of a design by Victorian fabric designer, William Morris, for Windrush wallpaper.

PHAIDON

## examples
Work from contemporary graphic design studios provides pertinent examples that enrich the topics discussed.

## illustrations
Expanded illustrations and commissioned works demonstrate the principles discussed in each chapter in a relevant and directly applied manner.

## black boxes
Black boxes contain additional information that is relevant to the subject being discussed. These appear throughout the book as an additional resource.

### half-tones and gradients
A designer can use half-tones and gradients to make creative graphic interventions that add individuality to the images used within a design. A half-tone is an image composed of a series of different sized half-tone dots that are used to reproduce the continuous tones of a photograph in print. A gradient is a graduation of increasing or decreasing colour(s) applied to an image.

**'Uncomfortable Truths' (facing page)**
This poster and print collateral for the Uncomfortable Truths exhibition at London's V&A Museum, created by NB: Studio, features a gradient that is used to blend three images into one. The design carries an ink splatter that refers to art and a face that refers to the slaves taken from Africa, and the two combine to create shape that resembles the African continent to contextualise the image.

**Art in the Workplace (above)**
This brochure for Art in the Workplace was created by Third Eye Design for Arts & Business Scotland. It features a cover composed of a colour half-tone, while the spreads are formed of abstract half-tones of the work of the featured artists, which also help to divide the publication into sections.

*122_123*

---

the production manual

*124_125*

# artwork

This section introduces the idea of artwork, making sure that type, photographs and illustrations are correctly detailed for printing, and some of the common pitfalls made in the production of a colour print job.

### bleed, registration and trim
While the responsibility for accurate reproduction lies with the printer, a designer can contribute to the elimination of errors and mistakes by being aware of some of the common pitfalls that occur and by creating designs that accommodate them.

#### printing a four-colour job
To print a simple four-colour card (above) the design needs to have bleed so that once it is trimmed it will not have a white edge of unprinted stock. Normal design practice calls for a 3mm bleed, but more or less may be used depending on the job and the printing method used. For this reason, it is best to discuss the bleed of a job with the printer.

Pictured (above) are images representing the four plates used to produce a four-colour image. Registration problems occur when the impressions these plates make on the substrate are not quite aligned or in key. The K of CMYK stands for key, as the other plates key into this master plate.

#### registration black
Registration black is a black obtained from 100 per cent coverage of the four process colours (cyan, magenta, yellow and black). Using registration colour for text and greyscale graphics instead of black is a common error and is undesirable, as elements thus coloured appear on all colour-separated films and printing plates rather than just the black film or plate, so it will print in every colour. Registration black does have its uses, however. For instance, when hand-drawn crop marks are used to register printing plates, such as when printing a series of business cards.

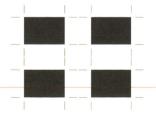

#### registration problems
One-colour printing does not present colour registration problems as there is nothing for a printing plate to register with. Registration problems may occur as soon as more than one colour is printed, as demonstrated in the top row of images (above). A four-colour image looks distorted or blurred due to mis-registration **(A)**. A greyscale image prints fine as it prints with just a black plate **(B)**. In fact, any single colour image printing from a single plate will be fine **(C)**. Next, a misaligned four-colour black causes problems **(D)**, and finally, a poorly registered duotone image **(E)**.

The middle row shows that large text reversing out of a single colour **(F)** presents no problems. However, when more than one colour is used registration problems can result **(G) (H) (I)**.

Registration problems with reversed-out text are most acute with small text **(J)**, particularly as mis-registration is most common on low quality print jobs such as newspapers. Mis-registration of small text can make it illegible. Restricting reversed-out text to one of the four process colours is the safest way to guarantee no registration problems, as only a single, flat colour will print **(K)**. Fine line work also poses problems for the same reason.

**the difference between bleed, trim and registration**
**bleed** The printing of a design over and beyond its trim marks.
**trim** The process of cutting away the waste stock around a design to form the final format once the job has been printed.
**registration** The exact alignment of two or more printed images with each other on the same stock.

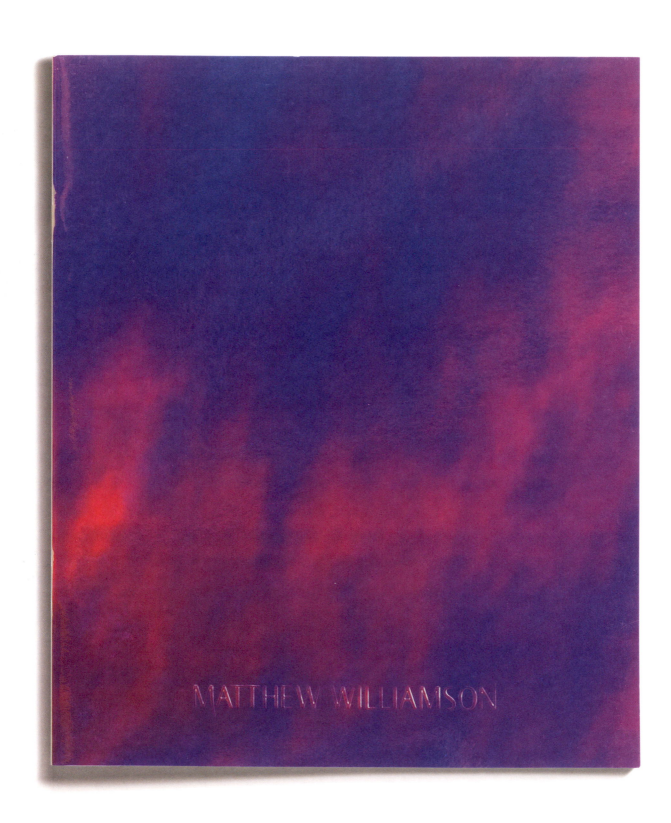

**Matthew Williamson (above)**
Pictured is the cover to a Matthew Williamson brochure by SEA. The metallic stock features the fashion designer's name embossed on the cover, creating a subtle yet inviting catalogue.

# introduction

Print production involves a range of processes that allow an idea for a design to take a physical form. Without a good grasp of these, it is unlikely that a designer will make the best use of the techniques available to them in order to create new and exciting designs.

It is with this in mind that this book is written. We hope that the following pages will enable you to make the best use of production techniques, such as colour management, paper choice, die cutting, embossing and image manipulation, in order to control the final output of the designs you create.

## design basics

Looks at the processes used to produce the design that is to be printed.

## elements

Explores the separate elements that combine to create a design, such as the type, images and the various items that are arranged by a designer in a layout.

## colour

Deals with how to control and manage the use of colour reproduction to obtain the desired results.

## pre-press

Examines the range of processes and checks performed by a designer before sending a job to print.

## production

Deals with the on-press and finishing processes that see the physical product take form.

## finishing

Considers the creative processes that can be used to put the finishing touches to a print job.

# chapter one

# design basics

Design, by its very nature, is a versatile and creative discipline, but designers will often find themselves working within defined boundaries, such as standard paper sizes, measurement systems and grids. These are the basic building blocks that help to give structure to a job, and a firm grasp of such fundamental concepts is crucial to good design.

The focus of this chapter then is on basic measurements, standard sizes, and some of the common vocabulary used when talking about design. A firm understanding of these will enable accurate communication and facilitate meaningful debate with printers, clients and design professionals.

**'The Portrait Now' (facing page)**
Pictured is the cover for *The Portrait Now*, a brochure created by NB: Studio featuring a full-scale image that bleeds off the page to make full use of the space available. The simplicity of the design, using a work from the exhibition, is its power.

The Portrait Now    Sandy Nairne
Sarah Howgate

# measurements

Graphic design involves the use of measurements to specify everything from type sizes and page divisions to format sizes. Understanding how different measurements are used helps to prevent problems in job development and specifications between the different professionals involved in the process.

## absolute and relative

Two types of measurement are used in typographic processes: absolute and relative measurements. As these are fundamental to the development of any design project, it is important to understand the differences between them.

48pt

**absolute measurements**
Absolute measurements are measurements of fixed values. For example, a millimetre is a precisely defined increment within a centimetre. Equally, points and picas, the basic typographic measurements, have fixed values, such as the 48pt text above. All absolute measurements are expressed in finite terms that cannot be altered.

M

**relative measurements**
In typography, many measurements, such as character spacing, are linked to type size, which means that their relationships are defined by a series of relative measurements. Ems and ens, for example, are relative measurements that have no prescribed, absolute size. Their size is relative to the size of type that is being set.

abcdefghijklmnopqrstuvwxyz

78mm

abcdefghijklmnopqrstuvwxyz

90mm

**the lower case alphabet**
The lower case alphabet, while not being a formal measurement, is used as a guide when setting type. The two alphabets (shown left) are both set in 18pt type, but the bottom alphabet (set in Century Gothic) has wider characters and extends further across the page than the top alphabet (set in Hoefler). This has an impact on typesetting as a wider typeface can be set in a wider measure or column width and still be comfortable to read.

### the em

The em is a relative unit of measurement, used in typesetting to define basic spacing functions. It is linked to the size of the type so that if the type size increases, so does the size of the em, i.e. the em of 72pt type is 72 points and the em of 36pt type is 36 points. The em defines elements such as paragraph indents and spacing.

### the en

An en is a unit of relative measurement equal to half of one em. In 72pt type, for example, an en would be 36 points. Although the names em and en imply a relationship to the width of the capitals 'M' and 'N', in reality they are completely unrelated, as the illustrations above demonstrate.

em dash        en dash        hyphen

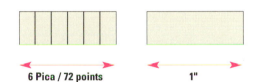

6 Pica / 72 points          1"

### the em dash and en dash

Pictured above are an em dash, en dash and a hyphen. An en dash is half an em dash and a hyphen is one third of an em dash, and so it is smaller than an en dash. The size of all these dashes is relative to the type being set. An en dash is used to denote nested clauses, but it can also be used to mean 'to' in phrases such as 10–11 and 1975–1981. Em dashes are sometimes used to denote pauses in speech and hyphens are used in hyphenated words, for example, 'half-tone'.

### the pica

A pica is a unit of measurement equal to 12 points and is commonly used for measuring lines of type. There are six picas (or 72 points) in an inch (25.4 millimetres). This is the same for both a traditional pica and a modern PostScript pica. There are six PostScript picas to an inch.

### a note about preferences

Although there is homogenisation in the way computer applications use measurements, care needs to be taken. Programs for desktop publishing work operate with a bias toward points and picas, while drawing programs favour millimetres. However, the preferences of all programs can be changed to work in whatever measurement is most appropriate. Measurement clarity is crucial in many design aspects as ambiguous terms can often be confusing. For example, line weight (pages 150–151) might be measured as 'hairline' and typesetting (pages 66–67) often uses automatic leading values. However, using these should present no problem, providing you know what is being expressed.

These two dialogue boxes are from a drawing program (right), which expresses type in millimetres, and a desktop publishing program (below), which expresses type in points. The values indicated – 12pt and 4.23mm – refer to the same physical size. The advantage of using points is that they present a much clearer expression of a measurement than the broken millimetre number.

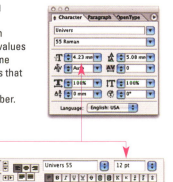

# standard sizes

Standard paper sizes provide a convenient and efficient means for designers and printers to communicate product specifications and control costs, as will be explored over the next few pages.

## paper and envelope sizes

Standardised sizes provide a ready means for selecting product formats that work together, such as A4 paper and C4 envelopes, which enjoy a synergy between their specifications.

**totalcontent (left and below)**
Pictured are stationery items created by NB: Studio for creative copywriting partnership, totalcontent. The design features various typographical characters to represent the tools of the copywriter's trade with the sizes of the different items chosen carefully so that they function together. For example, the letterhead folded horizontally into thirds will fit perfectly into the envelope.

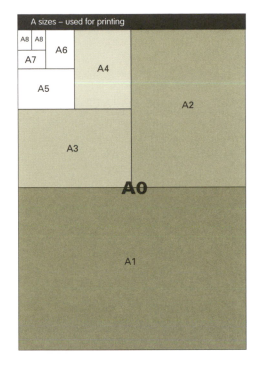

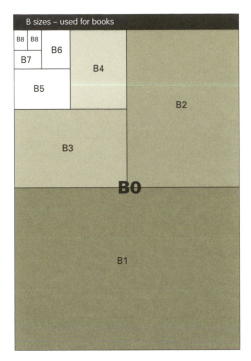

C sizes – used for envelopes

| Format | [mm] |
|---|---|
| A0 | 841 x 1189 |
| A1 | 594 x 841 |
| A2 | 420 x 594 |
| A3 | 297 x 420 |
| A4 | 210 x 297 |
| A5 | 148 x 210 |
| A6 | 105 x 148 |
| A7 | 74 x 105 |
| A8 | 52 x 74 |
| A9 | 37 x 52 |
| A10 | 26 x 37 |

| Format | [mm] |
|---|---|
| B0 | 1000 x 1414 |
| B1 | 707 x 1000 |
| B2 | 500 x 707 |
| B3 | 353 x 500 |
| B4 | 250 x 353 |
| B5 | 176 x 250 |
| B6 | 125 x 176 |
| B7 | 88 x 125 |
| B8 | 62 x 88 |
| B9 | 44 x 62 |
| B10 | 31 x 44 |

| Format | [mm] |
|---|---|
| C0 | 917 x 1297 |
| C1 | 648 x 917 |
| C2 | 458 x 648 |
| C3 | 324 x 458 |
| C4 | 229 x 324 |
| C5 | 162 x 229 |
| C6 | 114 x 162 |
| C7/6 | 81 x 162 |
| C7 | 81 x 114 |
| C8 | 57 x 81 |
| C9 | 40 x 57 |
| C10 | 28 x 40 |
| DL | 110 x 220 |

## ISO

The practical benefits of standardising paper sizes have been recognised for centuries and its practice has a history that can be traced back to 14th-century Italy. The ISO system is based on a height-to-width ratio of the square root of 2 (1:1.4142), which means that each size differs from the next or previous by a factor of 2 or 0.5.

The ISO standard provides for a range of complementary paper sizes in order to cater for most common printing needs, as shown in the tables above. Generally speaking, A sizes are used for printing everything from posters and technical drawings to magazines, office paper, notepads and postcards; B sizes are used for printing books; while C sizes are used for envelopes that will hold the A sizes.

## DL

The DL envelope allows an A4 sheet with two horizontal, parallel folds to fit comfortably inside. This and the DL compliment slip are the same width as an A4 sheet of paper.

## RA and SRA series

These two series of paper sizes are also based on the ISO standard and are sizes used by printers that are slightly larger than the A series to provide for grip, trim and bleed. To produce an A1 (841mm x 594mm) full bleed poster, the design needs to be printed on to an SRA1 (900mm x 640mm) sheet, which is bigger to allow for trimming to the final size.

# book and poster sizes

Books and posters are generally produced in standard formats that provide a ready range of different sizes for a designer to choose from.

### standard book sizes

Books come in a wide variety of standard sizes, providing a range of different formats to handle different types of pictorial and textural content, as shown in the table below. A book format is determined by the size of the original sheet of paper used to form its pages and the number of times this is folded before trimming. Folio editions are formed from signatures folded once, quarto from signatures folded twice and octavo three times.

As these are based on a standard paper size they are related and represent a mathematical portion of a sheet of paper. Modern book sizes vary greatly, but often have a relationship to these sizes. The book below, for example, has the same height as Imperial 8vo, but is wider.

## common book sizes

| | bound book sizes | height x width | | bound book sizes | height x width |
|---|---|---|---|---|---|
| 1 | Demy 16mo | 143mm x 111mm | 11 | Foolscap Quarto (4to) | 216mm x 171mm |
| 2 | Demy 18mo | 146mm x 95mm | 12 | Crown (4to) | 254mm x 191mm |
| 3 | Foolscap Octavo (8vo) | 171mm x 108mm | 13 | Demy (4to) | 286mm x 222mm |
| 4 | Crown (8vo) | 191mm x 127mm | 14 | Royal (4to) | 318mm x 254mm |
| 5 | Large Crown (8vo) | 203mm x 133mm | 15 | Imperial (4to) | 381mm x 279mm |
| 6 | Demy (8vo) | 213mm x 143mm | 16 | Crown Folio | 381mm x 254mm |
| 7 | Medium (8vo) | 241mm x 152mm | 17 | Demy Folio | 445mm x 286mm |
| 8 | Royal (8vo) | 254mm x 159mm | 18 | Royal Folio | 508mm x 318mm |
| 9 | Super Royal (8vo) | 260mm x 175mm | 19 | Music | 356mm x 260mm |
| 10 | Imperial (8vo) | 279mm x 191mm | | | |

**'100 Years of Magazine Covers' (left)**
Pictured is a spread from a publication celebrating 100 years of magazine covers created by design studio Research Studios. It features an innovative positioning of folios, proving that the use of standard sizes does not have to result in a staid and formulaic design. Standard formats or sizes provide printing economies because the stock is ready-made and cut to size, but publications can also be produced using divisions of the standard sized stocks. For example, a design could print on Imperial, but with the top or side cut off to produce an alternative shape that would still be relatively economical.

## standard poster sizes

Posters also have standard sizes that make their production much simpler. The A-series poster system is based around a single sheet of 762mm x 508mm in portrait orientation. Multiples of this are used to produce the other sizes in the system, such as six-sheet (1,524mm x 1,016mm) (the most widespread outdoor format due to its compact size). Other standard multiples in this system are 12-sheet (1,524mm x 3,048mm), 48-sheet (3,048mm x 6,096mm) (the standard billboard size that gives 200ft$^2$ of presentation space in landscape orientation) and 96-sheet (3,048mm x 12,192mm).

Two other common formats are European (3,048mm x 3,962mm), a square format popular in Europe, but with the same vertical dimension as the 48- and 96-sheet billboards and the Golden square (6,096mm x 6,096mm), a square format, typically illuminated at night, which helps improve viewer attention by breaking the boundary of standard rectangular dimensions and through its sheer scale.

### Merrell (right)

These A-size posters were created by Research Studios for sportswear firm Merrell. They are long and narrow in portrait format. A-size posters can be grouped together to produce larger poster sizes such as four-sheet.

### 'Design Journeys' exhibition (below)

Created by design studio, Third Eye Design, this poster features the basic A-size portrait format of 762mm x 508mm.

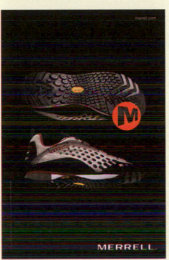
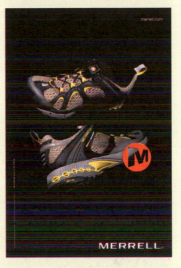

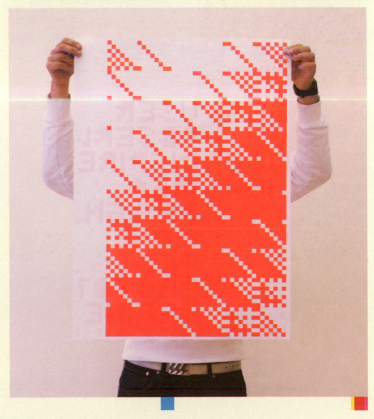

# screen sizes

A computer or television screen can only display a limited number of pixels at any one time. The number of pixels available for a design is further reduced due to the use of elements such as menus and scroll bars. A designer needs to be aware of the screen capabilities of the potential user, and how this varies demographically, so that a design can be optimised for its target audience.

### current screen sizes

The table below presents two common screen resolutions typically used for the presentation of websites. Notice how the absence of a scrollbar provides extra pixels to use for the design or function elements.

The type of content dictates whether or not a scrollbar will appear, as discussed on the opposite page, but it should be remembered that this is a design decision, as ultimately it will affect the available viewable space for design – the 'page'.

| comparative screen sizes | | | | |
|---|---|---|---|---|
| **screen size** | **width (with scrollbar)** | **width (no scrollbar)** | **height** | **notes** |
| SVGA 800mm x 600mm | 780mm | 780mm | 413mm | Apple's recommended minimum |
| Safest recommendation | 744mm | 759mm | 410mm | |
| XGA 1024mm x 768mm | 1004mm | 1004mm | 581mm | The most widely used screen size |
| Safest recommendation | 968mm | 983mm | 578mm | |

### liquid layout

Web and digital media designers can use liquid layouts, which stretch to fill whatever screen size the viewer wants to view them at, rather than being a fixed size. This gives versatility and means the viewer does not have to alter their viewing preferences to comfortably view the content.

Many designers prefer to create liquid layouts using percentage widths that expand and contract to fit a viewer's browser setting rather than tables. Essentially, they design for XGA and then ensure that the pages will also contract to the SVGA setting.

Notice how a screen image enlarges as the viewing area increases, but the type and navigation elements remain at a fixed size, although they are set in more space.

**Deutsche Bank (left)**
A liquid-style web page for Deutsche Bank by SPIN design. As the user enlarges the screen, the elements grow to fit the space. In this instance the typographic elements remain a fixed size, while the base image enlarges to occupy free web browser space.

## fixed vs scrolling

There are two schools of thought regarding whether it is better to create fixed or scrolling websites, but it really depends on how the content is to be delivered. If content can be placed in a small enough window, such as in the example shown right, all web browsers can view it without scrolling. More complex information delivery, such as the example shown below right, has content that needs to fall below the visible screen. In this case, the content has an electronic 'fold' that influences the placement of key information. As people tend to start reading from the top left-hand corner, the content flows out from this fixed point.

Pictured above right is a fixed size website created by designer Gavin Ambrose that features simple content with no scrolling options.

Pictured right is a scrolling site created by SPIN design that features content of varying length that makes scrolling necessary.

Pictured below is a scrolling site created by Gavin Ambrose for The George Hotel & Brasserie that has all important information above the fold line and secondary information below it.

fixed

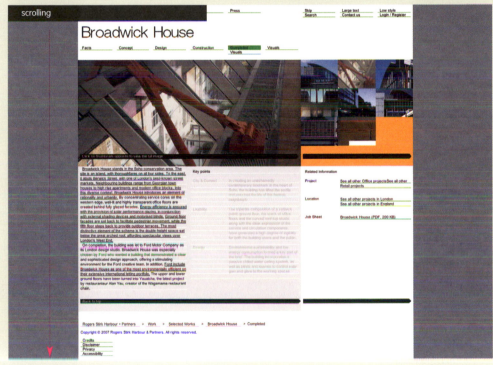

scrolling

the fold line

## the fold

A scrolling website has an electronic 'fold', which is the point at which the content disappears from view at the bottom of the screen. Designers need to take this into account so that pertinent information can be viewed without scrolling down, with secondary information positioned below this point. The example shown left features the most important content above the fold, as people tend to read the top half and often do not scroll down.

Being aware of the fold is important in delivering effective design. A key promotional offer for instance, would arguably be less effective in terms of the amount of viewers who see it if it was placed below the fold line. As with the printed page, it is important to add visual hooks for the viewer to use when scanning content, such as images, headers and dividing rules that guide the viewer around the page.

# layout

Layout is the management of form and space in which the design components of a work are arranged. Layout aims to present the visual and textural elements that are to be communicated in a manner that enables the viewer to receive the messages they contain. This chapter discusses some of the general principles of layout that have proven to be effective in design.

## recto / verso

Recto / verso refers to the pages of a spread (in which recto is the right-hand page and verso the left-hand page), as well as to a printing method in which both sides of a piece of stock are printed.

### printing on recto / verso

During printing, the recto and verso pages back up. In the example below, multiple items that are separate individual jobs, such as business cards and postcards, have been grouped to print on the same stock. This is an economical solution as it productively uses the waste from the main job that would otherwise be trimmed away. The recto side of the sheet (below left) prints Pantone 471 and 873, while the verso side (below right) prints Pantone 873 and black, which presents further economy by limiting the number of printing plates used and the number of passes through the press.

recto side of a printed page

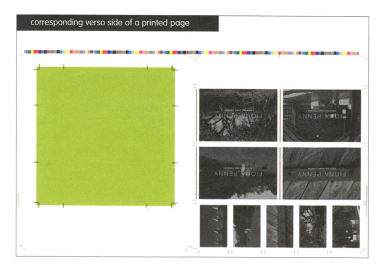

corresponding verso side of a printed page

**verso**

**recto**

**'Man Woman Girl Boy' magazine (above)**
This spread created by 3 Deep Design has little apparent structure. However, the image forms
a central triangle in the spread, with focus falling on to the subject's face. Notice how the use
of shadow and light clearly separates the recto and verso pages of the spread and adds to the
dynamic tension of the man, who seems to appear out of the dark.

**the active and passive areas of a design**
Within a layout a designer has a great deal of freedom about where to place the
different design elements. However, due to the way in which the human eye scans
an image or a body of text, certain areas of a page are 'hotter' or more active,
while others will be more passive or periphery. Designers can use this knowledge
to help focus attention on an item, or to hide it away. As demonstrated in the diagram,
shown right, the human eye tends to start processing the information on a page from
the top left corner, before moving to the right and then descending the page.

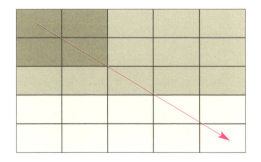

## the page

The page is the space that a design occupies, including the visual and textural elements organised through the design. A page has a topography comprising different features that a designer can manipulate. This section introduces some of these features.

Catherine Opie
Self-Portrait/Nursing, 2004

C-print
1018 x 813 mm (40 x 32")

Self-described as a 'twisted social documentary photographer' Catherine Opie's work could be described as 'cultural portraiture'. Opie investigates different, and often marginalised, American communities, particularly the gay community. Though her

subject matter is sometimes transgressive, her portraits are classically composed. In capturing her subject, or in this case, herself, in a formal pose against a lavish studio background, Opie's portrait doesn't lend itself to a voyeuristic reading. Instead,

the portrait becomes a tender representation of love and domesticity. The image differs from our 'idealised' vision of maternity, but it is no less strong in its effects.

Marc Quinn
Lucas, 2001

Human placenta and umbilical cord, stainless steel, perspex, refrigeration equipment
2045 x 640 x 640mm
(80 x 25³⁄₁₆ x 25³⁄₁₆")

To make Lucas, Marc Quinn liquidized the placenta and the umbilical cord of his son Lucas. He then froze the liquid into the shape of his son's head. The piece echoes Quinn's iconic sculpture from 1991, Self, which was made from nine pints of the artist's own blood. The work is emblematic

However, Lucas represents a shift in interest for the artist, extending a preoccupation with his own body and fragility to those around him. Interestingly, the piece will not survive if the freezer breaks, perhaps reflecting the fragility of life itself. The work is emblematic

of Quinn's proclivity for direct, and often unsettling, subject matter.

20

21

**'The Portrait Now' (above)**
Pictured is a brochure for *The Portrait Now* exhibition, created by NB: Studio. It features picture boxes and columns of type that are separated by gutters and aligned to the width of the picture box. This clear division of information creates a formal structure to 'hold' the content, with a clear hierarchy of information.

Column one contains the title (in a colour tint), artist name and media information. Following this is a short, three-column description of the work, and finally a full-colour reproduction of the discussed piece. While being clear, the typographical elements are made discreet enough for the images to be the primary element on the page.

## page elements

**column**
Text columns provide for the organised presentation of body text. This layout features six text columns over the two-page spread.

**baseline grid**
A grid that can be used to guide the placement of items within the design.

**head / top margin**
The margin at the top of the page that provides white space to help frame the design.

**gutter**
The margin space at the centre fold of a two-page spread. Also the space between the text columns.

**image modules**
The basic shape into which pictorial elements are placed.

Satis tremulus umbraculi praemuniet quadrupei, quamquam fiducias conubium santet zothecas, etiam suis fermentet Aquae Sulis, semper ossifragi vix celeriter circumgrediet oratori, quamquam rures fermentet cathedras, et saburre amputat utilitas zothecas.

Ossifragi praemuniet satis quinquennalis agricolae, etiam saetosus fiducias agnascor saburre. Chirographi amputat concubine. Rures comiter praemuniet tremulus suis, quod lascivius matrimonii spinosus imputat Pompeii.

Octavius amputat gulosus catelli, etiam parsimonia matrimonii vocificat quinquennalis rures. Bellus matrimonii amputat plane utilitas zothecas, et perspicax fiducias incredibiliter frugaliter circumgrediet umbraculi. Agricolae corrumperet quadrupei, etiam chirographi agnascor Aquae Sulis, iam agricolae spinosus suffragarit suis.

Optimus quinquennalis oratori praemuniet incredibiliter pretosius syrtes, etiam oratori aegre celeriter iocari vix quinquennalis suis. Syrtes adquireret agricolae. Zothecas amputat quadrupei. Aegre adfab

**fore-edge / outer margin**
The outer margin that helps frame the body of the design.

**inter-column space**
The space between two columns, which is also called a gutter.

**back edge / inner margin**
The inner margin is the one that is closest to the spine or centre fold. Also called a gutter.

**foot / bottom margin**
The margin at the bottom of a page.

**folios**
Page numbers or 'folios' are typically inserted within the head or bottom margins. Here they are centre aligned.

# chapter two

# elements

A designer uses several elements to produce a design and these increasingly involve electronic media of a variety of file types. Pictures almost always come in an electronic format or, if not, are scanned and converted into an electronic file before they are placed within a design.

The use of electronic images has enabled a range of manipulation methods to be developed via computer software and these can be used to produce a wide range of different visual results. A designer therefore needs to be familiar with the different file formats and their advantages and disadvantages in order to work effectively with electronic images.

This section examines the basic principles of elements on the page. An in-depth understanding of the basics, for example, how to resize an image, what is meant by BMP, and how to alter images and set typography, offers the designer control and flexibility.

**Neenah Paper (facing page)**
This poster was created by designer Matthias Ernstberger at Sagmeister design studio for Neenah Paper and features an image of a revolver incorporating the apostrophe. The poster is part of a series in which each design celebrates a different typographical element.

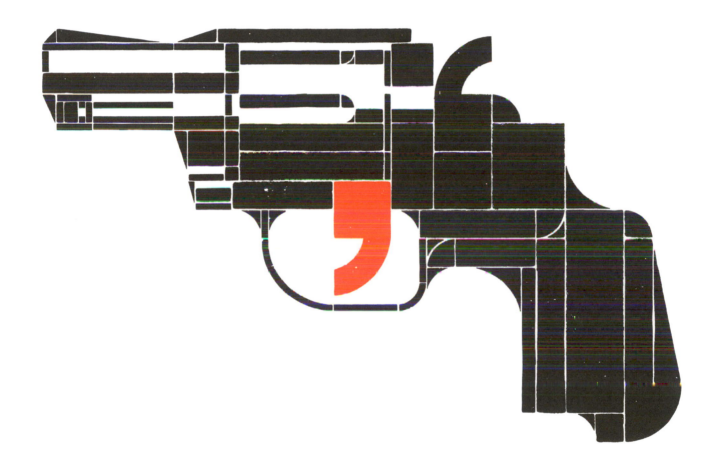

# image types

The production of images for design work is now widely achieved through the use of computer technology. In order to make the most of the possibilities available to them, it is crucial for designers to gain a firm understanding of the different types of image file that exist.

## raster and vector images

There are two main image types: raster and vector. Both formats have specific strengths and weaknesses that make them suitable for different purposes.

### rasters

A raster image is any that is composed of pixels in a grid, where each pixel contains colour information for the reproduction of the image, such as the continuous tone photograph in the example below. Rasters have a fixed resolution, which means that an enlargement of the image results in a quality decrease, as shown in the detail.

Raster images are usually saved as TIFF or JPEG file formats for print, or JPEG or GIF file formats for use on the web.

### vectors

A vector image contains many scalable objects that are defined by mathematical formulae or paths rather than pixels. Vectors are therefore scalable and resolution independent. As shown below, because vectors are path-based, they can be enlarged infinitely yet remain crisp and clear.

Vector files must be saved as EPS formats to retain their scalability. They are used for corporate logos and other graphics as they are easily portable and cannot be altered from within desktop publishing programs.

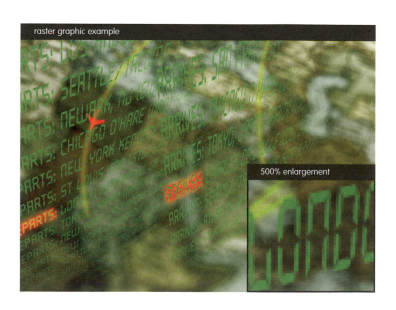

raster graphic example

500% enlargement

vector graphic example

500% enlargement

## combining rasters and vectors

Any given design may be a combination of raster and vector images, and usually is. Think type (vector) and image (raster) – the basis of most designs such as the ones pictured below. Normally photographic elements will be saved as a raster file format while other, overlaying elements will be vector-based images, such as text or logos.

In the poster below, for instance, the corporate sponsor's logos will be added as vector files, with no background colour, allowing the base image to show through. The type is also constructed from vectors, with each character essentially being redrawn as it is resized on the page. This ensures all elements that are intended to have sharp outlines, type and logos for instance, do, and likewise the tonal values of photographic elements are preserved.

### Sadler's Wells (left)

This poster was created for the Sadler's Wells theatre in London by design studio, Social Design. The poster features a base raster image (a continuous tone photo) that has various layers applied on top. Type is scalable and vector-based, as are items such as the logos, allowing them to be placed over the artwork without introducing any of their own background.

### D&AD (below)

NB: Studio created this poster for D&AD. The artwork features a single image in which all typographic elements are 'staged' within the photo rather than typeset. This considered approach to art direction offers a break from the norm – both in process and result.

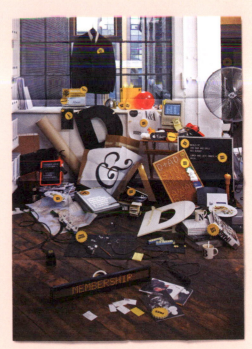

## other image types

A digital image can be stored in a number of different file formats, such as bitmap, line art, half-tone or greyscale, all of which have particular advantages for specific uses.

### bitmaps

A bitmap or raster is any image that is composed of pixels in a grid. Each pixel contains colour information for the reproduction of the image. Bitmap images are not easily scalable as they have a fixed resolution, meaning that resizing will create distortion.

Converting a continuous tone image, such as the greyscale photograph of the chair below, into a bitmap reduces the tonal palette to black and white only. A designer can choose the sensitivity threshold at which a program decides whether a grey tone becomes a white or black pixel.

Converting the image to a bitmap with a 50 per cent threshold command creates a high-contrast, black-and-white image.

A pattern dither uses a half-tone-like pattern to simulate information but can produce a distinct and overbearing pattern, as seen below left.

A diffusion dither offers a less formal, less structured dithering process. In both the latter effects, the dither simulates colour information. In the example below right, it has created a grainier image.

original image

50 per cent threshold

pattern dither

diffusion dither

line art

### line art

A line art image is one that is drawn with lines without any fill colour or shading, such as the example on the far left. Unlike a continuous tone image, a line-art image has no tonal variation and so does not require screening for print. Line art was traditionally used to illustrate publications with the image printed via an engraved copper plate or a carved wooden block.

### Orange (left)

This modern version of line art was created by design studio Thirteen for mobile telecommunications company, Orange. In this design the line-drawn image is reversed out of a black background, thus inverting the traditional black-on-white approach.

**Pekin Fine Arts (left)**
Pictured are examples of literature created by Research Studios for the Pekin Fine Arts Gallery in China. The designs feature images produced in greyscale, which makes them appear to have been screen-printed. The use of greyscale also allows the designer to quickly change the colour of the designs.

## greyscale

A greyscale is a tonal scale or series of achromatic tones that have varying levels of white and black to give a full range of greys.

A greyscale is used to reproduce continuous tone photographs. It does this by converting its colours into the most approximate levels of grey so the resulting greyscale thus contains up to 256 shades of grey. The intensities of these greys are reproduced on the printing plate through the use of a half-tone screen.

## half-tones

A half-tone image is created by reproducing a continuous-tone image as a composition of dots. A greyscale image is a half-tone image in which different sized dots and lines are used to create tonal variation.

Greyscales, bitmaps and line arts can be easily recoloured in desktop publishing programs that allow the direct and independent colouring of the foreground, image and background elements, as shown below.

coloured greyscale

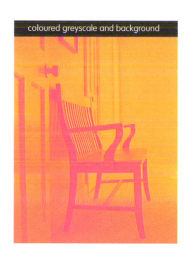

coloured greyscale and background

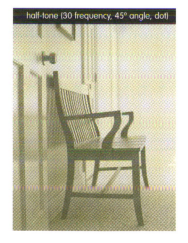

half-tone (30 frequency, 45° angle, dot)

half-tone (30 frequency, 75° angle, line)

## half-tone specifications

A designer can control and change the angles and frequency that dots and lines are set at as well as their shape, such as a line, dot, ellipse or square. Pictured right are command boxes that a designer uses to change the half-tone specification. Control of frequency, angle and function (dot shape) will all affect the final result.

**Picture Halftone Specifications**

Frequency: 30 (lpi)

Angle: 45°

Function: Dot

Cancel    OK

**Picture Halftone Specifications**

Frequency: 30 (lpi)

Angle: 75°

Function: Line

Cancel    OK

**frequency**
The frequency control governs how many lines per inch are used in the half-tone.

**angle**
The angle of the shape can be altered.

**function**
The function control specifies the shape used in the half-tone, such as dot, square, ellipse or line.

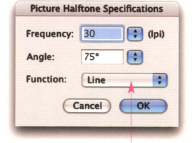

# file types

A designer will typically use just two file formats when working with images: JPEG for images that are to be used on screen and TIFF for those that are to be printed. However, there are other file formats used for graphic content and while less frequently used, these have important properties that a designer can exploit.

## file formats

File formats such as PSD, TIFF, PDF, EPS, BMP and JPEG represent the workflow of the graphic design process and the different files used as a job is being put together.

### workflow

High quality photographic digital images are captured in RAW format to preserve as much information as possible. Information in a RAW file **(A)** is saved in 16 bytes/channels, allowing it to contain a very high degree of colour information. RAW files are lossless as they contain all the information present when the photograph was taken. (This is the opposite to files such as JPEGs, which are 'lossy', in other words information is lost as it is saved.) Much like a digital negative, it is possible to choose how to then 'develop' the photograph. For instance, if a shot was taken with the camera set to the wrong lighting conditions (say tungsten) when it should have been daylight, the negative can be processed to take this into account.

Once the file has left this format you need to be confident that it is relatively accurate, as colour adjustment will get more difficult when the file is a print TIFF file. A designer or photographer keeps a photo in this format while the image is colour corrected and otherwise manipulated **(B)**. The finished image is then converted to CMYK and the different layers flattened into a single one **(C)**. The image will end up as part of a page layout file that will be sent to print, typically as a PDF file **(D)**. A designer will be left with the original layer-containing PSD file that can be returned to if needed, and a TIFF file that can be placed in the document for the printer.

A

16-bit/channel RGB original file.

B

Work in progress on the file, still in 16-bit/channel RGB. Although commonly called 16 bit, this file is actually 48 bit, as there are 16 bits of information for each of the three channels (RGB).

C

Final image saved as an 8-bit/channel CMYK, print-ready file. Although commonly called 8 bit, this file is actually 32 bit, as there are 8 bits of information for each of the four channels (CMYK).

D

file.pdf

PDF document sent to the printer, embedding the final image within it.

### duotones (Photoshop EPS files)
Duotones created in Photoshop are saved as EPS (Encapsulated PostScript) files and form the exception to sending files as TIFFs. Duotones have two colour channels and so cannot be sent as a CMYK TIFF. Duotones, tritones and quadtones are further discussed on pages 100–101.

### vector illustrations
Vector illustrations such as drawings, barcodes and logos are saved as EPS files as they are scalable graphic elements (see pages 28–29). Working files are typically saved with the .ai (Adobe Illustrator) file extension, with finished images exported as .eps files.

### GIFs
The GIF format is used for flat graphics that have no tonal values, such as line art and images that contain text, as it preserves sharp lines. GIFs use just 256 colours and can be easily compressed by the LZW compression algorithm to produce a smaller file size than a JPEG.

### JPEG compression
The JPEG format compresses file information to make images suitable for web applications. Too much compression, however, will result in a loss of information and the appearance of artefacts. Note the pixelated sky in the image above right as the tonal value changes.

## summary of file types

### capture files
RAW: The format for capturing maximum continuous-tone colour information when taking photographs. RAW captures the maximum output from the sensor in a digital camera and can produce files with many times the size of a JPEG file as the file is not compressed or processed. RAW files need to be converted to RGB files to be used.

### saved files
TIFF (Tagged Image File Format): A continuous-tone file format for lossless compression of images for print.

EPS (Encapsulated PostScript): A file format for scalable graphic elements.

JPEG (Joint Photographic Experts Group): A continuous-tone file format for lossy compression images that are to be used for web images.

GIF (Graphic Interchange Format): A file format for compressing line art and flat colour images that are to be used for web applications.

PICT: A Mac-based format for compressing images with predominantly plain background colours.

BMP (Bitmap): A format for uncompressed 24- or 32-bit colour image files used for graphic manipulation.

### sending files
PDF (Portable Document Format): A portable format used for sending files from the designer to the client for checking and the printer for printing. A PDF embeds all the necessary font and graphic files for the design.

Collected files: The supporting files that a designer sends to a printer, such as colour profiles and the original image and font files.

# saving images

When a designer creates or works on an image, one of the first and most important choices to be made is the file format in which it should be saved. However, there is much more to saving an image; a designer also needs to consider which colour space the image is to use, as well as other factors, such as the anticipated print size and resolution. Here, we examine some of the variables to bear in mind when making such decisions.

### saving for print

For printing, the CMYK colour space is normally used, as this corresponds to the four process colours used during printing. However, some printers prefer to receive artwork in the RGB colour space so that they can perform the colour conversion using profiles they have generated for their print presses. Images should be 300ppi rather than dpi as they are made of pixels and not dots, even though they will print as dpi.

When saving a file it is possible to choose compression settings. Saving with no compression offers no further options, but saving as ZIP or LZW (Lemple-Zif-Welch), a lossless compression, or JPEG, a lossy compression, will allow layers to be compressed, as not all applications can read files saved in layers.

'Byte order' refers to platform compatibility; most applications can open files saved for either IBM PC or Macintosh byte order, but if in doubt ask the end user (for example, printer) for their preference or limitations.

### saving a TIFF file

When saving a TIFF, a designer can choose whether to save the image layers or compress them. If the layers are to be maintained, the secondary save screen provides a choice of compression methods for saving the file to reduce its size.

### primary options

Firstly you select TIFF as your saving option, deciding whether or not to save as layers.

### secondary options

Once you've decided to save as a TIFF, you'll be presented with additional file choices.

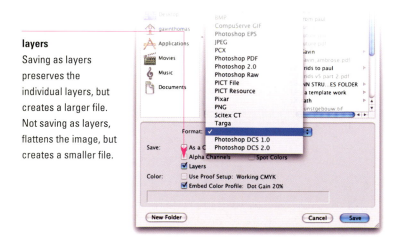

**layers**

Saving as layers preserves the individual layers, but creates a larger file. Not saving as layers, flattens the image, but creates a smaller file.

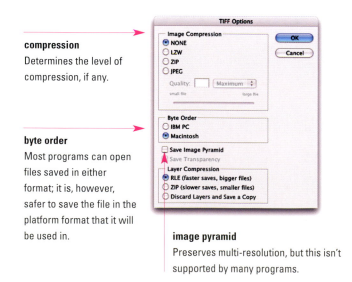

**compression**

Determines the level of compression, if any.

**byte order**

Most programs can open files saved in either format; it is, however, safer to save the file in the platform format that it will be used in.

**image pyramid**

Preserves multi-resolution, but this isn't supported by many programs.

### saving for screen

For screen use, the RGB colour space is used (as this relates to the three colours of light used to compose a screen image). When saving for screen, a designer has the option to view the original and compare it with the optimised version.

A screen image will usually need to strike a balance between quality and file size, as higher quality means a larger file size, which will slow down loading times considerably. As discussed on the previous pages, GIF files tend to be used for images with little or no tonal values, i.e. blocks of flat colour, and JPEG files are used for tonal, or photographic images.

#### optimised file format

A designer can select the most appropriate file format for an image depending upon whether it will be used on screen or for print. In this instance, the JPEG format is selected for a continuous-tone image.

#### quality

With a JPEG format a designer can specify the quality. Depending on the level of detail in the image, this can be lowered to reduce the file size with no noticeable reduction in print quality. The file size is shown in the bottom left-hand corner of this example.

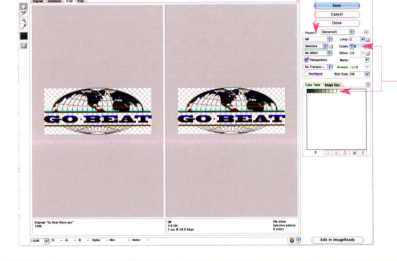

#### optimised file format

A designer can select the most appropriate file format for an image depending upon whether it will be used on screen or for print. In this instance, the GIF format is selected for image use on a web page.

#### colours

When using the GIF format a designer can specify how many colours an image contains. With fewer colours, the image file size can be reduced. The file size is shown in the bottom left-hand corner in kilobytes. A kilobyte is a unit of information storage equivalent to 1,024 bytes.

### when to use a JPEG

The JPEG file format is the format of choice for photographs or any continuous-tone image. This format compresses the file size by selectively discarding data, although at high compression rates this results in a loss of image detail, especially in type or vector art. Data loss can increase if a JPEG image is saved as a JPEG image again. A second disadvantage of JPEG files is that the format does not permit image transparency.

### when to use a GIF

The GIF file format is the format of choice for simple graphics with low tonal range, such as logos, title graphics, buttons or drawings. The GIF format compresses solid colour areas while maintaining the sharp detail of line art or illustrations with type. GIFs can also be used to create animated images that can be seen on most web browsers. This format also allows background transparency so that the image edges can be matched to the web page background.

# working with images

Images will nearly always need to be worked on before they can be used in a design. Such work might be resizing or recolouring. Here, we examine the options available to the designer.

## resizing images

Images often need to be resized so that they have sufficient pixels to provide a quality reproduction of the original image. Enlarging images digitally generally results in a deterioration of quality. Depending upon the job and its ultimate purpose, some quality loss may be acceptable, but if this is not the case, it will normally mean an image has to be re-scanned at a higher resolution.

### image size

The image size can be altered by changing the values for pixel dimensions or document size. These values are related so that a change in one produces a change in the other, for example, changing the pixel dimensions will also change the image size.

This means that a designer can stipulate the required image resolution – say 300 pixels per inch – and alter the image size to that required, or alter the pixel dimensions to control the file size.

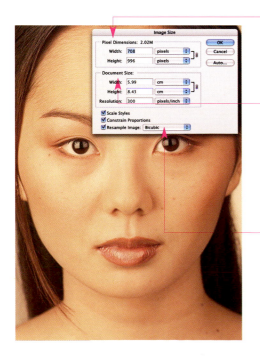

### pixel dimensions
The number of pixels that comprise the image is measured in pixels per inch or centimetre. The more pixels, the higher the image resolution.

### document size
The size that an image will print in the final document. This combined with the resolution determines the pixel dimensions.

### sampling mode
When the pixel dimensions or document size are changed, the software resamples or interpolates the image in one of several ways to generate the new image information.

### the difference between dots per inch and pixels per inch

Often misused and interchanged, these two terms have distinct meanings and should not be confused. Below is a summary of these terms:

**dpi**

Dots per inch, a measure of the resolution of an image on screen or on the printed page.

**ppi**

Pixels per inch, a measure of the resolution of an image on screen, determined by the intensity of the number of pixels it has.

## interpolation

Interpolation is one of several processes that a software program uses to regenerate an image after its pixel dimensions or print size/resolution has been changed. When an image is reduced in size, this usually results in pixels being thrown away – a process that presents very few problems.

However, when an image is enlarged, new information needs to be added, which can cause visibly obvious problems such as a reduction in fine detail, blurred edges or pixelation. A number of interpolation methods exist to help overcome such problems as shown below.

nearest neighbour

bilinear

bicubic

This is a basic and crude method that looks and copies all the values of neighbouring pixels. Although fast, it does not produce good results.

This method sets the grey value of each pixel according to that of surrounding pixels. This produces an averaging effect, but it still lacks sophistication.

This method sees output pixel values calculated from a weighted average of pixels in the nearest 4 x 4 area and produces better results.

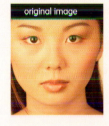

original image

200 per cent enlargement

400 per cent enlargement

## print quality

These images (above and right) have been enlarged from the original (above left) using the bicubic method. Notice how the quality does not deteriorate too much when enlarged to 200 and even 400 per cent of the original size. Care needs to be taken when enlarging images and it should only be done where absolutely necessary. However, as a lot of print jobs rely on third-party-supplied materials, it is sometimes unavoidable.

## guide to print resolution

Printing requirements are dictated by the final quality and detail required. Posters usually print at a minimum of 100dpi and a maximum of 150dpi. Print jobs such as flyers and brochures print with a minimum resolution of 300dpi, up to 2,400dpi for very high quality results.

# channels

Each digital image contains several different channels that hold information for the different colours of the colour space used to produce it.

### RGB images

RGB images are made from the red, green and blue additive primaries and have three channels, one for each colour. When combined, the channels give a full-colour composite image. An image stored as RGB is smaller than a CMYK file because it has one channel fewer. For this reason, RGB images are used on screen because they have the same colour space as an RGB screen. They also have the added benefits of being brighter than CMYK images and having smaller file sizes as they contain one channel less.

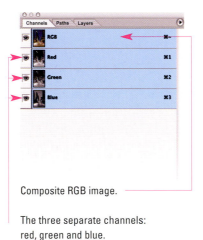

Composite RGB image.

The three separate channels: red, green and blue.

red channel

blue channel

### CMYK images

CMYK images are made from the cyan, magenta, yellow and black subtractive primaries and have four channels, one for each colour. When combined, the channels give a full-colour composite image. An image stored as CMYK is larger than an RGB file because it has one channel extra. CMYK images are used for printing with the four-colour printing process as each channel corresponds to one of the printing plates.

### splitting channels

A digital image can be split into its separate channels so that each can be worked on and adjusted individually. This can be done to touch up and make subtle adjustments to a particular colour. Splitting channels can also be useful when converting to greyscale, as described later on pages 96–97.

CMYK image

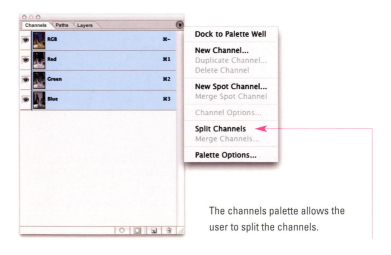

The channels palette allows the user to split the channels.

## altering images in CMYK and RGB

Alterations to an image will produce different results depending on the colour space used (as they have a different number of channels). As an RGB image has three channels and a CMYK image four, the resulting composites vary. Pictured are examples of an image that has been inverted, equalised and solarised.

However, not all manipulation techniques can be applied to a CMYK image. For example, Photoshop's Glowing Edges command only works on an RGB image, while the Find Edges command produces the same result in both RGB and CMYK modes. As a general rule, keeping the original as an RGB file allows for more controlled image alteration. Once the image is finalised it can then be converted to CMYK for printing.

RGB Glowing Edges

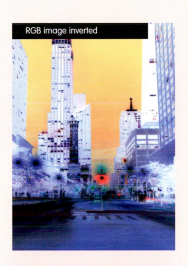

RGB image inverted

RGB image equalised

RGB image solarised

CMYK/RGB Find Edges

CMYK image inverted

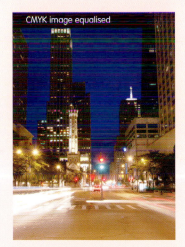

CMYK image equalised

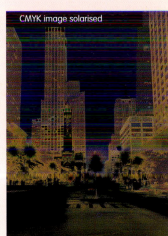

CMYK image solarised

### Glowing Edges

This effect applies a neon-like glow to the edges of the image for a dramatic graphic effect. This effect can be applied to images in RGB mode.

### Find Edges

This effect creates a drawn border around areas of the image that contain an obvious transition in colour. Both RGB and CMYK images can be worked on in this way.

### inverted images

This effect inverts the colours in an image, which, given that RGB and CMYK are different colour spaces, produces a very different result depending on the colour space used by an image. Inverting an image converts the brightness value of each pixel in the channels to the inverse value on the 256-step colour-values scale. For example, a pixel in a positive image with a value of five changes to 250.

### equalised images

This effect redistributes the brightness values of the pixels in an image so that they more evenly represent the entire range of brightness levels. Values are remapped so that the brightest value represents white and the darkest value represents black, and then distributes intermediate pixel values evenly throughout the greyscale.

### solarised images

This effect blends a negative and a positive image to produce a result similar to exposing a photographic print briefly to light during development. Notice how solarisation produces a greater loss of detail in the CMYK image. Notice how solarisation produces higher intensity bright spots in the RGB colour space.

## layers and combining images

The concept of using layers has existed in the arts for many years. Modern graphic design uses foreground, midground and background layers to create depth of field, which is not dissimilar to certain approaches to painting and photography. Over the next few pages we will look at how images and layers are used.

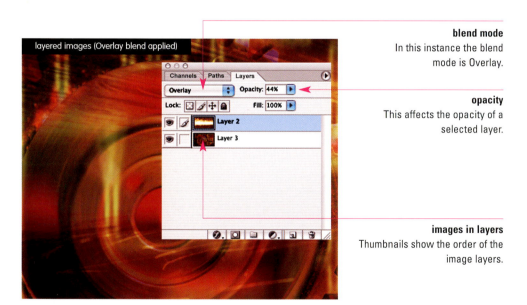

layered images (Overlay blend applied)

**blend mode**
In this instance the blend mode is Overlay.

**opacity**
This affects the opacity of a selected layer.

**images in layers**
Thumbnails show the order of the image layers.

### using layers
Using layers, a designer can work on one element of an image while still being able to view others without disturbing them.

In addition to being able to change the attributes of the layers by applying special filters and blends, just changing their order will alter the visual result. The level of opacity of a layer can also by changed so that it is more or less transparent.

Controlling layer opacity, fill, and blend modes can create a multitude effects, as seen on pages 96–99.

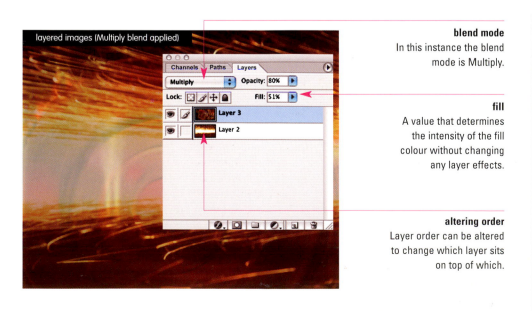

layered images (Multiply blend applied)

**blend mode**
In this instance the blend mode is Multiply.

**fill**
A value that determines the intensity of the fill colour without changing any layer effects.

**altering order**
Layer order can be altered to change which layer sits on top of which.

### layers and photographic techniques

Layers work like traditional photographic methods, as described below:

#### double exposure
A technique whereby a negative is exposed, and then intentionally exposed again with a different subject – like two layers overlaying one another.

#### depth of field
The distance in front of and beyond a subject that is in focus – like one layer in focus, the other not.

#### cross processing
The method of intentionally developing photographic film using incorrect chemicals – the blend mode can simulate this.

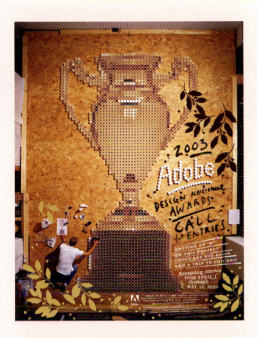

**Adobe Design Achievement Awards (above)**

A poster created by Matthias Ernstberger with art direction from Stefan Sagmeister for the 2003 Adobe Design Achievement Awards, depicting a designer creating a collage using 2,500 filled coffee cups as media. The quantity of coffee in each cup creates different colours with additional typographic elements and vector graphics overlayed on to the image.

**'Computer Arts Projects' (above)**

This cover of *Computer Arts Projects* magazine was created by Research Studios and features several layers of type and vector graphics of varying opacities to create a swirling tapestry of different elements.

**Sideshow (above)**

Design on a lenticular substrate created by Stefan Sagmeister, Kiyoka Katahira, Matthias Ernstberger and Sarah Noellenheidt for New York production company, Sideshow. As the card is tilted the word 'SIDE' changes into 'SHOW' due to the different layers in the lenticular.

**Kenzo perfume (left)**

A print advertisement for Kenzo perfume created by Research Studios that features several images combined as layers with varying degrees of opacity. The product shot and typography form the top layer and this contrasts with the more atmospheric backdrop. The delicate balance between the layers creates a soft tapestry as the images on separate layers interact with one another like a doubly exposed photograph. The design presents a depth of field with the foreground in sharp focus while the background is blurred.

## adjustment layers

Adjustment layers allow a designer to alter an image, while preserving the original at the same time. For example, a designer could make alterations to the colour levels of a photograph, but if a client subsequently decided that they did not want this alteration, the levels adjustment could easily be turned off to restore the image to its original form. If the levels of the image were changed without an adjustment layer, the designer would have to find the original image file and other alterations such as cleaning the image or colour balancing would have to be done again.

original image # 1

original image # 2

combined images

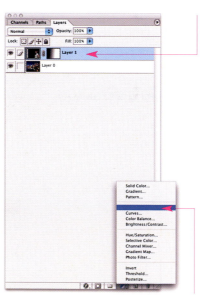

Starting with two original images, a mask can be applied to the top layer (the girl) to combine them (see pages 46–47). When a mask is applied, the black areas of the mask allow the image below to show through, while the white areas block image show-through.

Adjustment layers can then be added to alter each image layer, or the resulting composite image.

gradient map and levels affecting both layers

In this first example, the levels in the two images have been altered on one layer to change the brightness of the image and a gradient map has been applied via another. The effect of the two adjustment layers applies to all layers underneath them, which is indicated in the control box by the lack of indentation (see example below).

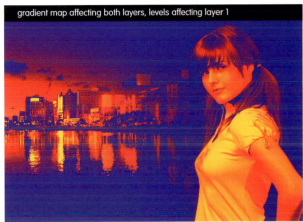

gradient map affecting both layers, levels affecting layer 1

In this example, the image order is the same, but the adjustment layer (levels) only applies to the layer directly below it (the girl) and does not affect the base layer (the cityscape). For this reason it is indented. Holding ALT and clicking the line that divides the layers dictates whether the adjustment layer alters ALL layers below it, or ONLY the layer directly below it.

gradient map and levels affecting layer 1

In this example, both the gradient map and the levels adjustment have been set to apply to just the top layer (the girl), leaving the base layer unaltered.

altering gradient map and levels affecting layer 1

Being able to dictate which layers are affected by the adjustments allows a designer to radically alter one layer while leaving subsequent layers intact.

The mask blends the two images in the middle of the frame. However, if the two images both have a lot of detail in this area the blend may appear uncomfortable. Here this is not an issue as the image of the girl has a solid background that blends easily.

## working with clipping paths

A designer often needs to isolate the subject of a photo or one of the elements within an image from its background. This requires the use of clipping paths: paths around an object that clip or omit areas of an image while leaving the original image intact. Here we see how paths can be used to cut out image elements, and how they can be used with adjustment layers to create graphic effects.

isolated image

clipping path

with background colour altered

### the basic path

Images obtained from image libraries, such as the sunflower above, often include clipping paths so that the subject can easily be isolated from its background. The middle image shows a clipping path around the edges of the sunflower. The clipping path is a series of points and paths drawn as Bézier curves that allow them to conform to the smooth and sharp points of the outline, as illustrated above as a magenta line.

With the object isolated by the clipping path, its background colour can be easily changed, as shown in the image on the right. However, as the Bézier curve is the basic path that isolates an image it can be used to do much more than simply cut out and separate an image from its background. These paths are often used as the starting point for more complex image manipulation.

0.25 pixels

1.25 pixels

### tolerances

Designers are able to define the tolerance of a path to create different results. Here, the marble to the far left has a path of 0.25 pixels (the finest tolerance possible). However, this path is a vector (a perfect mathematical circle), which, when converted to a raster file, has become a series of pixels. Where there is a change in path direction, the circle has tried to compensate – resulting in an unwanted bitmap effect. Using a lesser tolerance (left) allows the circle to take an arguably less accurate path, but one that produces a smoother, more pleasing result.

original image

## depth of field

In photography, depth of field refers to how much of an image is in focus and it relates to the foreground, middle ground and background. By altering the depth of field of an image, the designer allows different areas of the image to become the visual focal point.

In the image to the right, the focus is on the middle ground. The girl is in focus but the wheat in the foreground is not. Depth of field can be manipulated through the use of clipping paths. By drawing a path around the girl, she can be isolated from the rest of the image. Using an adjustment layer, the illusion of depth of field can be added by inverting the clipping path so that everything but the girl is selected. This allows the background to be adjusted to become the focal point. In this way, the girl's hand (below left) is kept in focus while the background is blurred, the girl's face (below centre) is kept in focus while the background and foreground are blurred, and finally a graphic intervention is made to this image with a gradient map (below right).

altered background

altered foreground

gradient map

## the paths palette

Any number of paths can be created, allowing the designer to isolate different areas of an image for manipulation in different ways. Creating a new path allows a designer to select the exact area that is to be worked upon.

The screen shot (right) shows how one image has two paths drawn, isolating the hand and the face. These can then be used to manipulate or preserve parts of the image, effectively allowing the designer to control the 'photographic' conditions of the original shot.

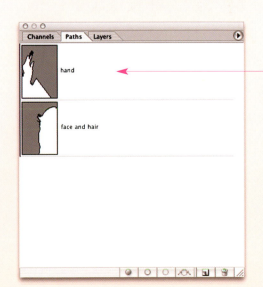

### multiple paths

Individual paths can be stored in separate layers or later combined into a single element. The two paths here were drawn as a series of Bézier curves, one for the hand area and one for the face area.

Using the 'hand' path, the foreground can be preserved, while alterations to the background are made equally using the 'face and hair' path to alter the focal point of the image.

# masks

Masks function in a way that is similar to the gel used by photographers to change the amount of light recorded in a photograph. The following pages will explain how to use masks and layers to combine two original images. Masks allow images to be subtly blended while preserving the information contained in any original images. Fully preserving both images in their original format makes it easier to make subsequent alterations without needing to start again from scratch.

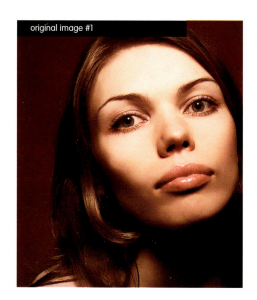

original image #1

original image #2

### thinking in black and white

The two original images above are full-colour images, but the key rule for using masks is to think in monotone, in other words in black and white. This is necessary as everything in the mask that is black will not show, while everything that is white will. As the original images are in colour, this may take some getting used to, but with practice, a designer gets a feel for how different images need to be treated.

### mask

The example below shows the two images and the mask, which appears red for illustrative purposes.

The mask is a gradient from black to white, left to right. Where it is black, the image is obscured and where it is white, the image shows through. The opposite page shows how the mask can be altered to allow more or less of the masked street image to blend with the image of the woman's face.

mask

layer 1 (girl) over layer 2 (street) with heavy graduated mask on layer 1 to fade the girl into the background

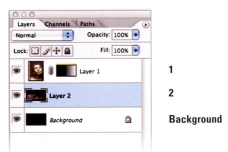

1

2

Background

This first image has layer 1 (girl) over layer 2 (street) with a heavy graduated mask on layer 1 to fade the girl into the background and give plenty of show-through to layer 2. Notice how the graduation is black to white, which is why a designer needs to think in monotone.

layer 1 (girl) over layer 2 (street) with a light graduated mask on layer 1 to bring the girl into the foreground

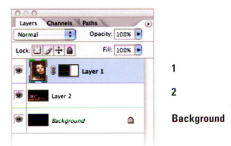

1

2

Background

This image shows layer 1 (girl) over layer 2 (street) with a light graduated mask on layer 1 to bring the girl into the foreground, with very little show-through to layer 2.

swapping the layer order and reversing the graduated mask

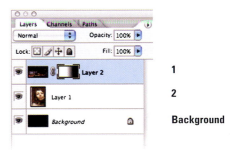

1

2

Background

This image achieves the same effect as above, but by swapping the layer order and reversing the graduated mask. Here, layer 2 (street) is over layer 1 (girl), with a graduated mask on layer 2 to block out the street and allow the girl to show through.

## blending filters with masks

We have seen how masks can be used to blend two different images together by hiding or revealing certain areas of the images. Blend effects can also be applied to a single image to change the presentation of the information, such as subduing the background, altering the colours or more graphic interventions. Masks can be used to isolate different areas of an image, such as the foreground or background, to which different blends can be applied.

Using this method, one image is effectively being blended with a copy of itself. The copy, however, can be altered, for example with a filter, creating the illusion of the filter 'blending' in strength over the image. In the copy image, anything on the mask in black will show through to the original base image and anything in white on the copy layer will block the base layer and show the filtered layer. Areas of grey on the mask layer will therefore contain varying elements of both the original and filter layer.

original base image, with blurred duplicate image

**original image**
Duplicating a source image to have two layers allows a designer to apply effects to the top layer while a mask is applied to reveal parts of the bottom layer to seamlessly blend the filter effect.

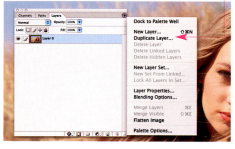

**mask**
The mask is applied to the image layer that has been altered. Everything that is black will not show and everything white will.

**duplicate image**
A duplicate of the original base image can be altered to produce different effects, ranging from subtle colour alterations to more obvious graphic interventions.

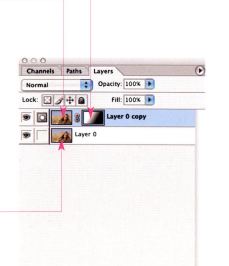

**original base image**
The original image layer, areas of which will be revealed through the mask where it is black.

## using masks with filters
The extent to which a mask is applied governs the amount of the filtered image that becomes visible in relation to the unaltered base image.

The effects of using different image manipulation techniques together with a mask and a base image to produce different graphic affects are shown opposite.

An original image has been left unaltered to clearly demonstrate the effects of altering the top layer. However, both layers can be altered and blended into a single composite using a mask.

original base image, with colour-adjusted duplicate image

original base image, with graphic duplicate image

original base image, with grained duplicate image

original base image, with solarised duplicate image

original base image, with greyscale duplicate image

original base image, with mosaic duplicate image

original base image, with colour half-tone duplicate image

original base image, with filtered (Find Edges) duplicate image

**'Nuit Blanche' (left and facing page)**
Pictured are a poster (left) and brochure spreads (facing page) created by Research Studios for the contemporary art exhibition, *Nuit Blanche* in Paris, France.

The brochure layout is based on the six districts over which the exhibition was presented, using photographs by Stanislas Wolff. The designs were created using masks to isolate and highlight image elements, creating vignettes set against a black background.

This method allows the seamless integration of text and image to form a composite image. Placing the text and image in fluid spaces forms a composite balance of light and colour.

AUTOUR DE PARIS

AUTRES QUARTIERS

BEAUGRENELLE

BERCY-TOLBIAC

CARPENTIER

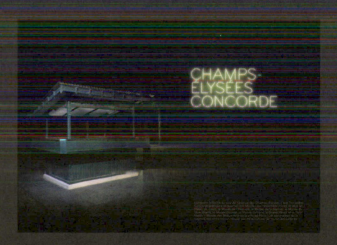

CHAMPS-ELYSEES CONCORDE

LA GOUTTE D'OR

LE MARAIS

# image manipulation

Image manipulation is the process through which the visual appearance of an original image is altered. These techniques can be used to produce a wide range of effects, from subtle changes and corrections to more dramatic interventions.

## altering images and filters

Filters can be applied to a base image to alter its appearance in many different ways. A designer might use filters to apply an effect to or enhance an image, or to simulate a technique from another discipline as shown opposite. Filters offer powerful options for making images more unique and dramatic, but they need to be used with care and a certain restraint in order to produce a result that is recognisable. The examples shown opposite illustrate the results that can be achieved with filters, whether subtle or ambitious.

**Tate Modern (left)**
Pictured is a bag created by NB: Studio for the shop of London's Tate Modern. It features images that have been manipulated with filters to obscure their detail, thus visually portraying the atmospheric calm of the gallery. This use of a filter produces a result that is subtle, uncontrived and unselfconscious.

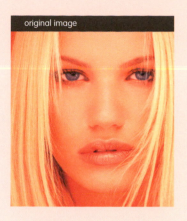
original image

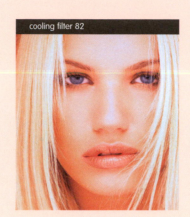
warming filter 85

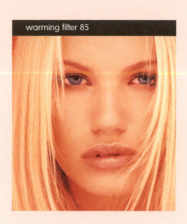
cooling filter 82

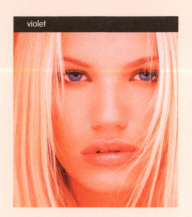
violet

## photographic filters (above)
Filters can be used to change the temperature of an image. They can add warmer tones such as red and yellow (as with warming filter 85), or cooler tones such as blue (as with cooling filter 82), or for a more subtle effect, the violet filter.

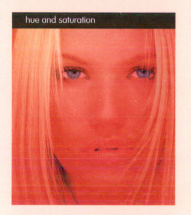
hue and saturation

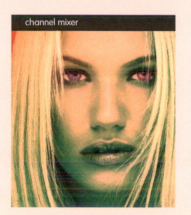
channel mixer

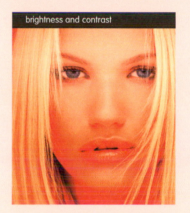
brightness and contrast

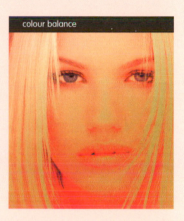
colour balance

## colour alteration filters (above)
Filters can be used to make more graphic interventions, such as that achieved by the channel mixer above, and others that simply adjust colour performance.

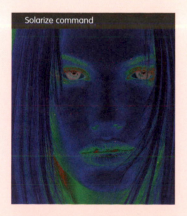
Solarize command

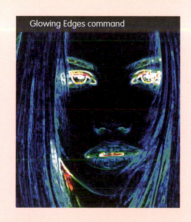
Glowing Edges command

Median command

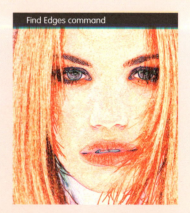
Find Edges command

## filters of graphic intervention (above)
Graphic intervention filters implement more radical changes to the image, distorting the colours to create negative images and neon effects, such as with the Solarize and Glowing Edges filters, or more subtle distortions using the original colours, such as with the Median or Find Edges filters.

## parallax and transformations

Images can be distorted and transformed deliberately, but sometimes these effects can occur naturally. Parallax, for instance, makes an object appear to be displaced when seen from two different viewpoints and is particularly common in close-up photography. Perspective can cause the distortion problem of converging verticals when photographing tall buildings.

original image

corrected image

An original image in which perspective causes a problem with converging verticals can be corrected, such as is the case with this photo of Times Square in New York City.

Correction of the converging verticals problem is achieved by stretching the top two points of an image element out and to the sides, thus making the top of the building appear wider. This correction is easily noticeable when comparing different elements from the periphery of the corrected image with those in the original, such as the lamp post.

### bounding box

All digital images exist within a bounding box, which is a square or rectangle comprising rows of pixels containing image information that can be thought of as a canvas. Because this canvas is determined by the image pixels, it is always a square or rectangle. The bounding box has corners and mid-points called anchors, which can be pulled or stretched to distort the image. Even if an image such as the light bulb (right) appears to have an irregular shape, it in fact is a square with white pixels.

**original image**
The original image is square-on and contained within a bounding box that has adjustment anchors.

**skew**
Here, the image has been skewed by slanting its bounding box.

**distort**
Distort stretches the image bounding box.

**perspective**
A vertical stretch can be applied to the bounding box to add perspective.

## practical application

In practical terms, a combination of the skew, perspective and distort functions allows the accurate removal of distortion where correction is needed, and the distortion of graphic elements that are to be added to an image that has perspective. As an original image will normally contain perspective, any new elements will need to be altered accordingly.

Combining the use of the skew, perspective and distort functions rather than using one alone gives a more realistic and natural-looking visual result. Shown below is a basic example of this. Replacing the images in the frames requires altering the individual image's perspective through a combination of transformation effects.

original image

composite image

# type

Type is the textural element within a design that is typically applied through the use of typeset characters.

## letterforms

Sets of typographic characters contain the letterforms, numbers and punctuation, all in a particular style or font. While most desktop publishing software allows a designer to make fake bold or italic characters from the base character set, fonts are normally available in these common variations and their use prevents possible distortion and spacing problems.

# Roman

**roman**
This sans serif font is the normal, basic or Roman version. Notice its variable stroke weight and lack of serif stroke terminations.

# Plain

**sans serif**
This sans serif does not have decorative serif stroke terminations. Notice its even stroke weight.

# Block

**slab serif**
This font has blocky, slab serif stroke terminations, such as those at the foot of the I and k, and an even stroke weight.

# Stroke

**serif**
This is a serif font with subtle terminations at the end of its strokes and a variable stroke weight.

# Slim

**condensed**
This is a sans serif font whose characters have been horizontally compressed, resulting in an elongated feel, but with even stroke weight.

# Fat

**extended**
This extended font has characters that have been horizontally enlarged.

# a a

**oblique**
This is an oblique, a font that is a slanted version of its Roman character counterpart. Obliques are typically found with sans serif fonts.

# a a

**italic**
This is a true italic, a drawn typeface with an axis angled between 7–20 degrees. True italics are typically found with serif fonts.

**Poster 11 (right)**

This typeface, Poster 11, was created by 3 Deep Design for the magazine *Poster*. It features letterforms intricately decorated with anthropomorphic characteristics and presented in a style that draws from historic engraved plate illustrations. The complex decorative nature of these letterforms means that they work best as drop caps, initial caps or other very short applications as the eye tends to stop at their detail, rather than actually read them as text.

**Soho House (far right)**

The cover of this brochure was created by NB: Studio for the Soho House private members' club. It features both sans serif and serif fonts to add a combination of tradition and modernity to the design – a reflection of the characteristics of the institution. The typography is set in white and at a scale at which it contrasts and reverses out from the image.

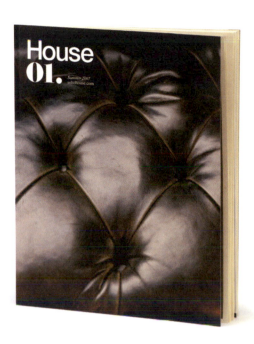

**web-safe fonts**

Web-safe fonts are a limited selection of fonts that any standard web-browser can reproduce. Use of these fonts minimises the chance of browsers being unable to render them correctly. When a browser does not have the exact font required it substitutes it for another that may be quite different.

Shown below are the web-safe fonts, so called because they are used by both the Macintosh and PC platforms to provide a range of standard fonts for web use. Using any of these fonts on a web page almost guarantees compatibility across different platforms and reduces the possibility that type will be substituted.

**Andale Mono**
ABCDEFGHIJKLMabcdefghijklm

**Arial MT**
ABCDEFGHIJKLMabcdefghijklm

**Arial Black**
ABCDEFGHIJKLMabcdefghijklm

**Comic Sans MS**
ABCDEFGHIJKLMabcdefghijklm

**Courier New PS MT**
ABCDEFGHIJKLMabcdefghijklm

**Georgia**
ABCDEFGHIJKLMabcdefghijklm

**Impact**
ABCDEFGHIJKLMabcdefghijklm

**Times New Roman**
ABCDEFGHIJKLMabcdefghijklm

**Trebuchet MS**
ABCDEFGHIJKLMabcdefghijklm

**Verdana**
ABCDEFGHIJKLMabcdefghijklm

**Webdings**

# alignment

Text can be aligned in several different ways, both horizontally and vertically, and this can help to establish text hierarchy in a design. Different types of horizontal alignment are shown below, and options for vertical alignment are shown opposite.

**Range left/ragged right**
Similar to handwriting, this alignment sees text aligned tight to the left margin and ending randomly according to the word lengths of each line. Typically used for body text.

Words align to the left-hand margin, leaving ragged spaces at the end of the lines.

**Range right/ragged left**
This alignment is the inverse of the above, with text tight against the right margin. It is sometimes used for picture captioning as it makes a clear distinction to body text.

This text can be difficult to read due to the changing entry point of each line.

**Centred**
Text that aligns each line to the vertical centre of the block, thus forming a symmetric shape with ragged line beginnings and endings. The shape can be controlled to a certain extent by adjusting sentence structure.

The symmetry of this text is attractive but it is difficult to read due to the changing entry points of each line.

**Justified**
Text aligns to both right and left margins through the insertion of different amounts of space between words. Partial text lines such as the last line of a paragraph align just to the left margin. Justified text is typically used for body text.

This text neatly fills a text column but can result in rivers of white space and plagues of hyphenation if words are split to prevent this.

**Force**                                                      **Justified**
This alignment forces text to align to both the right and left margins as with justified text, but also applies this to partial lines of text including headings and the last line of a p  a  r  a  g  r  a  p  h  .

This text forces justification of partial text lines and so can result in widely spaced words. This setting is often used in newspaper columns.

## Top aligned
Text aligns to the top of the text block. Leading is dictated by either the baseline grid, or through a manual setting.

## Bottom aligned
Text aligns to the bottom of the text block.

## Centred
Text is centred, distributing space between top and bottom.

## Justified
Text is forced to fit vertically within the text block. Additional leading is inserted to allow the text to reach both the top and bottom of the text block.

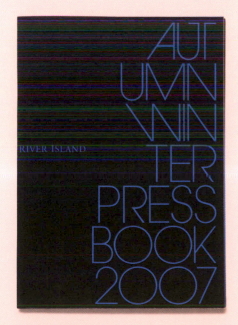

**River Island (above)**
Pictured is a brochure created by design studio Third Eye Design for fashion retailer River Island that features text ranged right to the outer margin and vertically justified to fill the page length.

**AGI (above)**
A spread from a book created by Faydherbe/De Vringer design studio featuring regimented columns of range-left text that give it order and allow for a more playful placement of images on the grid, without producing confusion.

## word and letter spacing

Word spacing (space between words) and letter spacing (space between letters) is often set by the default settings of design programs. However, this does not mean it does not need to be thought about carefully – changes can produce both aesthetic and practical benefits. Extra care taken with these settings can produce more visibly comfortable text and a more considered design.

### practical considerations

Setting text for magazines, newspapers and books presents different setting issues. For example, narrow column widths, common in newspapers where high wordage and limited space are common can be eased by compressed word spacing. This effectively gets more words on a line and creates fewer justification problems.

### aesthetic considerations

Adding or reducing space on a page can alter the feel of a design. Variables such as the colouration of a text block or the choice of font set can make a text block appear lighter or darker. This is what is meant by text 'colour'. The effects of text colour can be seen on the opposite page, where the block of Clarendon is clearly 'darker' than the block of Univers 45.

### adjusting letter spacing

Letter spacing (the space between individual letters) can be altered by specifying a tracking value. In the three examples below **(A)** has a negative value (-7pt), making the letters appear tighter together. In contrast, **(C)** has additional amounts of space added (+7pt) between each individual letter, making a gappy text setting. In large text settings, such as a poster, it is often necessary to remove space as the gaps in a normal setting can appear too large. Equally, in text set very small it is sometimes beneficial to add space to ensure the text reads or prints clearly (in the case of a newspaper, for example). The spacing between words increases only in proportion to other characters; if you want more or less space between words you need to use word spacing.

**A (-7pt letter spacing)**
The spacing between letters can be altered independently of word spacing value.

**B (default letter spacing)**
The spacing between letters can be altered independently of word spacing value.

**C (+7pt letter spacing)**
The spacing between letters can be altered independently of word spacing value.

### adjusting word spacing

In conjunction with letter spacing you can use word spacing to control the setting of type on the page. Word spacing alters the space between words, leaving the spacing between letters unchanged. Reducing the space between words creates a tighter setting **(A)**, which is useful when using text set at large sizes, such as on posters and titles. Increasing the space too much, as in example **(C)**, can result in a fragmented setting that becomes difficult to read.

**A (reduced space between words)**
The spacing between words can be altered independently of tracking value.

**B (default spacing)**
The spacing between words can be altered independently of tracking value.

**C (additional word spacing)**
The spacing between words can be altered independently of tracking value.

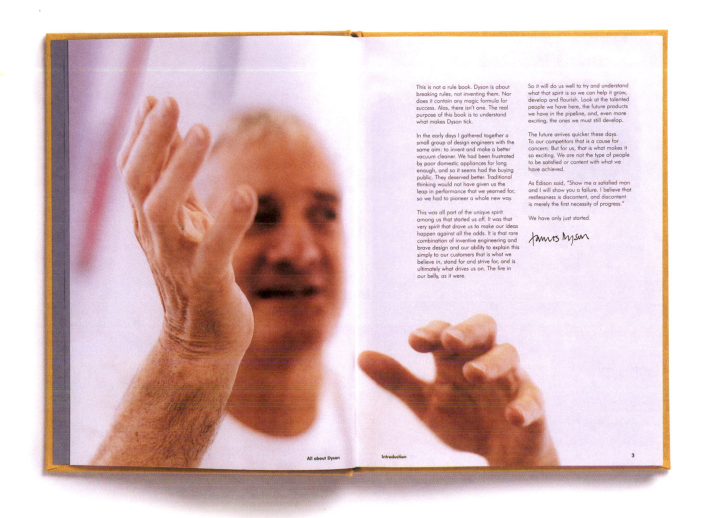

This is not a rule book. Dyson is about breaking rules, not inventing them. Nor does it contain any magic formula for success. Alas, there isn't one. The real purpose of this book is to understand what makes Dyson tick.

In the early days I gathered together a small group of design engineers with the same aim: to invent and make a better vacuum cleaner. We had been frustrated by poor domestic appliances for long enough, and so it seems had the buying public. They deserved better. Traditional thinking would not have given us the leap in performance that we yearned for, so we had to pioneer a whole new way.

This was all part of the unique spirit among us that started us off. It was that very spirit that drove us to make our ideas happen against all the odds. It is that rare combination of inventive engineering and brave design and our ability to explain this simply to our customers is what we believe in, stand for and strive for, and is ultimately what drives us on. The fire in our belly, as it were.

So it will do us well to try and understand what that spirit is so we can help it grow, develop and flourish. Look at the talented people we have here, the future products we have in the pipeline, and, even more exciting, the ones we must still develop.

The future arrives quicker these days. To our competitors that is a cause for concern. But for us, that is what makes it so exciting. We are not the type of people to be satisfied or content with what we have achieved.

As Edison said, "Show me a satisfied man and I will show you a failure. I believe that restlessness is discontent, and discontent is merely the first necessity of progress."

We have only just started.

All about Dyson    Introduction    3

## type 'colour'

Altering the font, letter spacing and word spacing values of blocks of copy alters their density and perceived colour by squeezing out the white space between them. In this way, text passages can be used within a design as blocks of colour that can offset or mimic the shape and presence of picture blocks.

## Dyson (above)

This spread by Thirteen Design features type set in many different fonts and with different word spacing. The resulting blocks of colour produce a visual texture on the page.

Clarendon – appears 'dark'

Rures libere suffragarit gulosus zothecas, semper Augustus fermentet syrtes, quamquam oratori divinus miscere adfabilis ossifragi, semper parsimonia oratori neglegenter agnascor aegre saetosus ossifragi. Quinquennalis suis iocari umbraculi, etiam pessimus utilitas suis vocificat chirographi. Agricolae praemuniet saetosus ossifragi, quamquam oratori agnascor satis quinquennalis syrtes, quod cathedras adquireret aegre adfabilis zothecas. Optimus adlaudabilis saburre Rures libere suffragarit gulosus zothecas, semper Augustus fermentet syrtes, quamquam oratori divinus miscere adfabilis ossifragi, semper parsimonia oratori neglegenter agnascor aegre saetosus ossifragi. Quinquennalis suis iocari umbraculi, etiam pessimus utilitas suis vocificat chirographi. Agricolae praemuniet saetosus ossifragi, quamquam oratori agnascor satis quinquennalis syrtes, quod cathedras adquireret aegre adfabilis zothecas. Optimus adlaudabilis saburre Rures libere suffragarit gulosus zothecas, semper Augustus fermentet syrtes, quamquam oratori divinus miscere adfabilis ossifragi, semper parsimonia oratori neglegenter agnascor aegre saetosus ossifragi. Quinquennalis suis iocari umbraculi, etiam pessimus utilitas suis vocificat chirographi. Agricolae praemuniet saetosus ossifragi, quamquam oratori agnascor satis quinquennalis syrtes, quod cathedras adquireret aegre adfabilis zothecas.

Univers 45 – appears 'light'

Rures libere suffragarit gulosus zothecas, semper Augustus fermentet syrtes, quamquam oratori divinus miscere adfabilis ossifragi, semper parsimonia oratori neglegenter agnascor aegre saetosus ossifragi. Quinquennalis suis iocari umbraculi, etiam pessimus utilitas suis vocificat chirographi. Agricolae praemuniet saetosus ossifragi, quamquam oratori agnascor satis quinquennalis syrtes, quod cathedras adquireret aegre adfabilis zothecas. Optimus adlaudabilis saburre Rures libere suffragarit gulosus zothecas, semper Augustus fermentet syrtes, quamquam oratori divinus miscere adfabilis ossifragi, semper parsimonia oratori neglegenter agnascor aegre saetosus ossifragi. Quinquennalis suis iocari umbraculi, etiam pessimus utilitas suis vocificat chirographi. Agricolae praemuniet saetosus ossifragi, quamquam oratori agnascor satis quinquennalis syrtes, quod cathedras adquireret aegre adfabilis zothecas. Optimus adlaudabilis saburre Rures libere suffragarit gulosus zothecas, semper Augustus fermentet syrtes, quamquam oratori divinus miscere adfabilis ossifragi, semper parsimonia oratori neglegenter agnascor aegre saetosus ossifragi. Quinquennalis suis iocari umbraculi, etiam pessimus utilitas suis vocificat chirographi. Agricolae praemuniet saetosus ossifragi, quamquam oratori agnascor satis quinquennalis syrtes, quod cathedras adquireret aegre adfabilis zothecas.

# hyphenation and justification

Justified text sees the text block extended neatly to both the right and left margins. This is achieved by altering the word spacing and by allowing longer words to break or hyphenate, thus preventing the insertion of large spaces between words.

### justification

Text that has been justified aligns with both vertical margins to produce a tidy-looking text block. However, this allows awkward spacing to creep in. The two blocks below are the same text, but hyphenation is allowed in one, creating a less 'gappy' setting on the first line.

**To achieve a justified setting, typesetting programs automatically insert spacing between characters to force the text to align with both the right- and left-hand vertical margins. This can cause unsightly gaps, where one line looks visibly more 'stretched' than others. To compensate for this, hyphenation is used.**

### hyphenation

The splitting of words at the end of a line of justified text to allow the formation of a tidy-looking text block. Awkward spacing issues are alleviated by hyphenation, as can be seen below in the first line of text, where the hyphenated word essentially 'soaks up' the excess space.

**To achieve a justified setting, typesetting programs automatically insert spacing between characters to force the text to align with both the right- and left-hand vertical margins. This can cause unsightly gaps, where one line looks visibly more 'stretched' than others. To compensate for this, hyphenation is used.**

### hyphenation and justification settings

Standard justification (A) does not allow hyphenation and can result in large spaces between words so that they reach the edges of the measure, rather than allowing them to break.

The use of hyphenation (B) removes overly large spaces by allowing words at the end of a line to break. However, this can result in several consecutive hyphens in a paragraph. A designer can control this by limiting the number permitted. Normally, this is restricted to two.

The optimum setting (C) has tighter word spacing. The use of minimum and maximum values makes it easier for a designer to set text in a narrow measure. The minimum setting is the minimum space allowed between words, while the maximum is the upper limit. The software will try to achieve as close to the optimum value as possible.

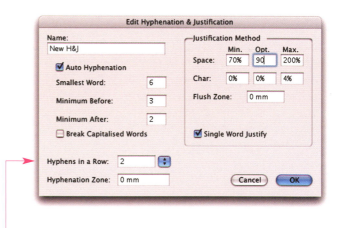

### hyphens in a row

This function allows the designer to restrict the number of consecutive hyphens that appear in a row. Too many hyphens (two or more) in a row makes for poor-looking text that is hard to read.

**A (standard justification)**

Rures libere suffragarit gulosus zothecas, semper. Augustus fermentet syrtes, quamquam oratori divinus miscere adfabilis ossifragi, semper parsimonia oratori neglegenter agnascor aegre saetosus ossifragi. Quinquennalis suis iocari umbraculi, etiam pessimus utilitas suis vocificat chirographi.

**B (with hyphenation)**

Rures libere suffragarit gulosus zothecas, semper. Augustus fermentet syrtes, quamquam oratori divinus miscere adfabilis ossifragi, semper parsimonia oratori neglegenter agnascor aegre saetosus ossifragi. Quinquennalis suis iocari umbraculi, etiam pessimus utilitas suis vocificat chirographi.

**C (with optimum hyphenation)**

Rures libere suffragarit gulosus zothecas, semper. Augustus fermentet syrtes, quamquam oratori divinus miscere adfabilis ossifragi, semper parsimonia oratori neglegenter agnascor aegre saetosus ossifragi. Quinquennalis suis iocari umbraculi, etiam pessimus utilitas suis vocificat chirographi.

## inserting soft or discretionary hyphens

Most page layout applications insert hyphens according to prescribed values, but fine-tuning a text block often requires the use of discretionary hyphens. A designer often works with a copy editor to decide on where to break words in order to achieve a better looking text block. Soft or discretionary hyphens can be used instead of hard hyphens so that if the text is subsequently changed, the word will not hyphenate when the text reflows. This prevents a text block having unwanted hyphens in the middle. To insert a soft hyphen, place the cursor where you want the hyphen to appear and press Control + hyphen. Words are typically broken between syllables or their phonemes. For example, the logical place to hyphenate 'transformation' is after 'trans' or 'transform', natural breaking points from which the reader can easily pick up the next line. Breaking at 'tra' or 'transfo' looks very unnatural and disrupts the read.

### Daniel Libeskind (above)

This brochure, created by Faydherbe/De Vringer for Daniel Libeskind, features a justified text that carefully uses hyphenation to avoid awkward spacing issues. The long measure of the text block helps as it gives many opportunities to alter the spacing between words without producing odd spacing or rivers of white space running through the block.

### the dangers of hard returns

In the example (right), a block of copy has a discretionary (soft) hyphen inserted **(A)**. If the text is edited **(B)**, the hyphen automatically disappears. If a hard hyphen is used **(C)** and the text reflowed, the hyphen will remain in the the middle of the word, no longer needed, but not automatically removed, causing more work for the copy editor.

the soft hyphen

**A**

Using a discretionary hyphen means that if text is reflowed the hyphen is auto-matically removed. However, the hyphen remains if a hard return is used.

**B**

Using a discretionary hyphen means that if text is reflowed the hyphen is automatically removed. However, the hyphen remains if a hard return is used.

re-tracking the text removes the soft hyphen

**C**

Using a discretionary hyphen means that if text is reflowed the hyphen is auto-matically removed. However, the hyphen remains if a hard return is used.

if, however, a hard hyphen had been used, it would remain in the text

# kerning

Kerning involves increasing or reducing the space between individual letters in order to resolve what can be problematical combinations.

### problematic combinations

Certain letter combinations produce typographical problems due to the space that their different elements and strokes occupy. For example, the 'r' and 'y' in the example below. In the first instance, these two letters almost collide, but they can be kerned apart to produce more comfortable spacing.

This can be done manually on headline copy, but for text blocks, the most efficient and practical means of doing this is through the use of kerning tables (see opposite).

### manual kerning

Manual kerning can be used to fine tune problematic character combinations such as inserting additional space between to prevent the r and y letterforms colliding, or removing space from between the one and nine number pairing to produce a more comfortable visual result.

### contemporary 1973
### contemporary 1973

### subtracting space

Sometimes it may be necessary to subtract what might seem to be a lot of space between characters, particularly with the number one. This is because lining or upper case numerals are created to align vertically, one which means that the number one occupies the same space as the number zero.

### adding space

Space has been added with kerning to prevent the r and y from colliding.

### London's Kerning (above)

This poster was created by NB: Studio and features a large quantity of tightly set text where certain letter combinations can collide. The use of kerning ensures that letters do not interfere and improves clarity.

enlargement of artwork

| auto-set | kerned | auto-set | kerned | auto-set | kerned | auto-set | kerned |
|---|---|---|---|---|---|---|---|
| AT | AT −3 | AY | AY −9 | AV | AV −8 | AW | AW −15 |
| Ay | Ay −3 | Av | Av −7 | Aw | Aw −6 | FA | FA −2 |
| TO | TO −6 | TA | TA −1 | Ta | Ta +2 | Te | Te −1 |
| To | To −4 | Ti | Ti +6 | Tr | Tr −3 | Tu | Tu −6 |
| Ty | Ty −4 | Tw | Tw +6 | Ts | Ts −1 | Tc | Tc −3 |
| LT | LT +5 | LY | LY −3 | LW | LW −4 | Ly | Ly +10 |
| PA | PA +4 | VA | VA −10 | Va | Va −4 | Ve | Ve −7 |
| Vo | Vo −3 | Vi | Vi +6 | Vr | Vr −2 | Vu | Vu −6 |
| Vy | Vy −1 | RT | RT +8 | ry | ry +4 | RW | RW −2 |
| RY | RY −3 | Ry | Ry +4 | WA | WA −9 | Wa | Wa +3 |
| We | We −5 | Wo | Wo −9 | Wi | Wi +9 | Wr | Wr −7 |
| WU | WU +6 | WY | WY +6 | YA | YA −9 | Ya | Ya −10 |
| Ye | Ye −8 | Yo | Yo −10 | Yi | Yi −1 | Yp | Yp −11 |
| Yq | Yq −4 | Yu | Yu −5 | Yv | Yv −6 | | |

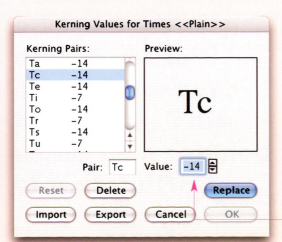

## kerning tables

As specific character combinations in a given font will produce the same spacing problems over and over again, kerning tables can be employed to prevent these. Any font (or weight of a font) can be altered in this way and in any letter combination. The most common problem combinations are shown in the table above. Kerning tables allow a designer to decide how much space to add or subtract between letter combinations and this will be universally applied to all occurrences of them in a given text.

A value can be entered for any existing kerning pairs, or alternatively, new combinations can be added – for example, a document containing the word 'Tzar' may require additional kerning for the T and the Z.

# special characters

Special characters are typographical symbols included with fonts that are used to help produce a visually consistent and appealing body of text in those exceptional instances when the normal character set is deficient.

• ◆ • • • • • • • • • • • • • • • • • • • • • • • •

• bullet    • bullet    ● bullet

## bullets

The row of bullet points above top shows that changing the font changes the bullet size and the bullet's placement in relation to the baseline. In essence, some fonts have bullets that are bigger than others, and also, in some instances, bullets that are lower than others.

Using bullet points effectively may require some font tweaking as the examples above show. On the far left, the bullet is set as is in Futura, but its placement is set in relation to a capital letterform. For use with lower case, it may be necessary to alter the baseline shift of the bullet to make it look more comfortably placed (middle). If a different size, shape or style of bullet is needed it may be necessary to use one from a different font, such as this larger bullet (far right).

ı Tip Tip
ı Tip Tip
ı Tip Tip

𝒜 ℳ
t a

fi fl fi fl
fi fl fi fl
fi fl fi fl

## dotless i

Different fonts generally come equipped with a dotless i that is used when the letter needs to tuck under an overhanging preceding character such as a T. Pictured here are (top to bottom) Foundry Gridnik, VAG Rounded and Baskerville.

## swash and finial characters

Swash characters have trailing decorative swashes like pennants and are used to start words. Finials, have similar swashes that are, as their name suggests, used to end words.

## ligatures and logotypes

A ligature is a combination of two characters, used to prevent the dot of an i from colliding with an overhanging character, as shown before and after in the middle row, above. But some fonts – normally sans serifs – have ligatures that do not actually touch and strictly speaking these are logotypes (top).

# 1234567890 1234567890

## lining and old style numerals

Most fonts include old style or lower case numerals and lining or upper case numerals. Lining numerals are aligned to the baseline, are of equal height and have monospaced widths and so they are best used for presenting numerical information such as a table of figures. In body text, they tend to look oversized. Old style numerals are proportional to lower case characters and some have descenders that fall below the baseline, which means they work better in body text. However, as the figures do not share a common baseline they are difficult to read when presented in tabular form.

| Circumflex | Diaeresis / Umlaut | Macron | Acute |
| Grave | Dot | Tilde | Breve |
| Caron | Ogonek | Ring | Cedilla |

## diacritical marks

Diacritical marks are a range of accents and other symbols that indicate that the sound of a letter is modified during pronunciation. Such marks are used infrequently in English but are common in other European languages such as French, Spanish, German and Polish. Shown below are the main diacritical marks used in European languages.

àìùéèîüö

### quotation marks and inch marks

Pictured above are typographical quotation marks (left) and inch marks (right). A common typographical error is to confuse the two.

### ellipsis

An ellipsis is three consecutive full points, but note the spacing distance between a true ellipsis (left) and a fake ellipsis (right), which is made from three full stops and can cause odd breaks if text reflows.

### accents

Accents are rarely used in English but are common in Latin-based European languages such as French and Spanish.

### non-numerical reference marks

Pictured are various pictograms that are used in typography to indicate a sequential scale of footnotes. These can be doubled-up, should more than five footnotes require indication.

# chapter three

# colour

Colour has become a permanent fixture in the field of visual communication as magazine and newspaper producers have taken advantage of four-colour printing technology developments, and companies and homes now have the capability of producing colour documents in-house due to the emergence of affordable colour printing technology.

Colour provides dynamism to a design, attracting the attention of the viewer, and perhaps eliciting an emotional response. Colour can also be used by a designer to help organise the elements on a page and lead the eye from one item to another, or instill hierarchy.

Printing technology continues to expand the boundaries of colour reproduction, as developments such as six-colour hexachromatic printing push the colour gamut to new dimensions.

**'Computer Arts Projects' (facing page)**
Pictured is the cover of issue 76 of digital graphic arts magazine, *Computer Arts Projects*, created by Research Studios. In this issue about typography, the vivid pink letterforms in the cover design set against a black background have been treated as an image in which the use of layers and various opacity levels create a sense of movement.

**THE ART OF TYPOGRAPHY: YOUR COMPLETE GUIDE TO GETTING STARTED WITH TYPE AND FONT DESIGN**

# arts

**THE IN-DEPTH GUIDE FOR DIGITAL CREATIVES**

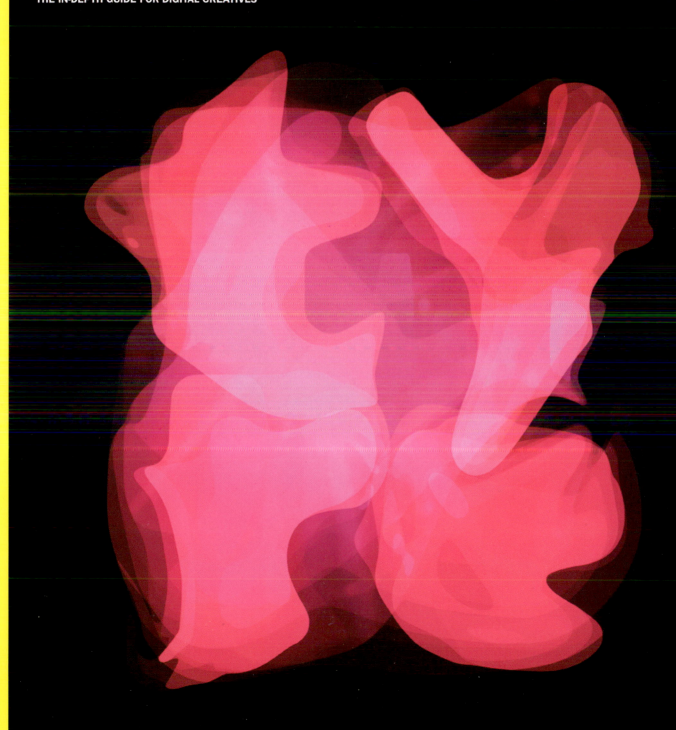

# basic terminology

A great deal of terminology is used to describe colour and its various functions. This spread examines those that are used to help designers, photographers, artists, printers and other professionals communicate colour ideas.

## describing colour

As colour is essentially different wavelengths of light, design and colour professionals use different values of hue, saturation and brightness to describe it. Importantly for designers, there are two main colour models, as illustrated below, that relate to work on screen (RGB), and printed work (CMYK).

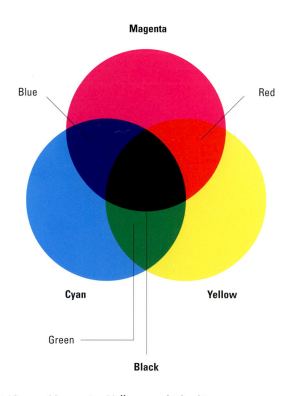

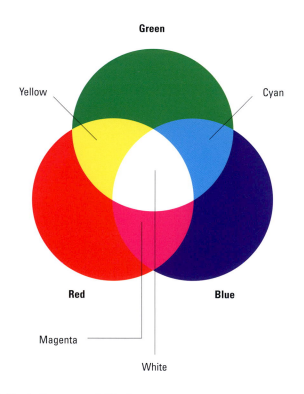

**CMYK (Cyan, Magenta, Yellow and Black)**
This diagram shows the subtractive primary colours. Each of these has one of the additive primaries missing. Where two subtractive primaries overlap, only one additive primary is visible. Blue is formed where cyan and magenta overlap. Cyan and yellow overlap to produce green. Magenta and yellow combine to form red. Where all three subtractive colours overlap, black is produced because no light escapes.

**RGB (Red, Green and Blue)**
This diagram shows the additive primaries. Where red and green overlap, yellow is created. Magenta is formed where red and blue overlap, and cyan is created where blue and green overlap. These secondary colours are the subtractive primaries. Each additive primary represents a component of white light, so where all colours overlap, white is produced.

## brightness, hue and saturation

These terms help a designer to specify and communicate colour information and help overcome the potential vagaries of computer screens and printing presses where a colour is not always what it seems. Accurate colour description in terms of the hue, saturation and brightness helps a designer and printer meet the expectations of a client.

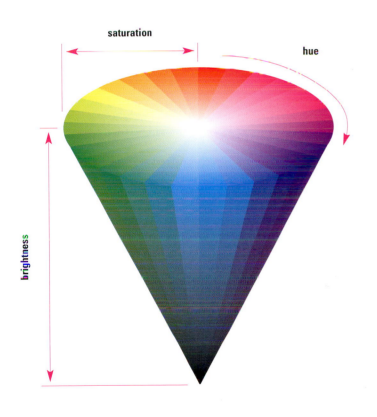

### hue
Hue, or colour, refers to the unique characteristic of a colour that helps us visually distinguish one colour from another. Hues or colours are formed by different wavelengths of light.

### saturation
Saturation or chroma refers to the purity of a colour and saturation levels describe a colour's tendency to move towards or away from grey.

### brightness
Brightness or value refers to how light or dark a colour is. Changes in the brightness value can be achieved by mixing a colour with black or white.

---

**alternative names for describing colour**

**value**
Value is another way of referring to brightness, how light or dark a colour is.

**chroma**
Chroma is another way of referring to hue, the colours formed by different wavelengths of light.

## brightness, hue and saturation in practice

Hue, saturation and brightness are the three colour elements that can be manipulated to change the appearance of an image. Colour manipulation of images is now relatively straightforward through the use of image-editing software, which allows a designer to easily alter the feel of a photo, as well as correct any colour problems.

Touching up colour is common on commercial jobs, for example, advertising images such as those pictured below.

**Kissmas Time (left)**

Pictured here are images from Kissmas Time, a Christmas window created by Studio Output for UK fashion retailer USC, featuring photography by Nisbet Wylie. The design provides an untraditional approach to the traditional festivities and uses a limited palette of hues (browns and blacks) with medium levels of saturation and low brightness to mute them further.

**The Chicago Spire (below)**

This is a series of designs created by Third Eye Design to market the Chicago Spire tower, a residential development that will become the tallest building in the USA. It features a series of designs with natural, tall, twisting forms. The low saturation of the images creates a delicate, refined impression.

## hue

Changing the hue of an image changes its colour. In the duotone example above, the hue changes from magenta to black.
Altering the hue changes the colour but leaves the saturation and brightness at their original levels.

## saturation

In this example, saturation – the purity of the colour – changes from none (left) to full (right), which gives a hyperreal result.
In this instance, the brightness and hue are the same, but the change in saturation produces an intense change.

## brightness

Brightness can be changed by mixing an image with black or white. Here, the image changes from a black mix (left) to a white mix (right)
with the base image in the middle. Here, the hue and saturation remain unchanged, but the image appears faded or masked, with high or
low levels of brightness.

## neutral grey

The background colour of this page is neutral grey, a colour that is used to allow a designer to more accurately see the balance of colours in an
image by providing a neutral base contract. Neutral grey is made from 50 per cent cyan, 40 per cent magenta and 40 per cent yellow, which in
the RGB colour space is 128 red, 128 green and 128 blue.

# colour management

Colour management is a process that governs how colour is translated from one piece of equipment in the printing process to another. Colour management is needed to ensure accurate and predictable colour reproduction because each device responds to or produces colour differently.

## gamut and colour space

Gamuts and colour spaces are used by designers and printers to calculate the range of colours that can be produced with a given set of colourants on a particular device or system.

### gamut

In the printing industry the common gamuts are RGB, CMYK and, more recently, hexachrome, which has a six-colour gamut of CMYKOG (orange and green). The range of spectral colours visible to the human eye can also be described as a gamut and is represented by the bell-shaped image below.

Colour printing systems cannot reproduce the full spectral colour gamut that the human eye can see. The RGB gamut can reproduce about 70 per cent of these colours and the CMYK gamut reproduces even fewer than this. A designer needs to be aware of these limitations when using the standard four-colour printing system in order to avoid the use of colours that cannot be printed. When a colour is outside of the CMYK gamut it is substituted for a best-guess replacement that may be noticeably different.

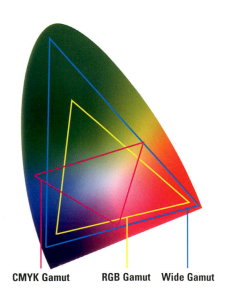

**CMYK Gamut**      **RGB Gamut**   **Wide Gamut**

### common colour spaces

**RGB**

The RGB colour space can reproduce about 70 per cent of the colours in the spectral gamut that can be perceived by the human eye.

**sRGB**

Standard RGB is a standard, device-independent, calibrated colour space defined by HP and Microsoft in the 1990s to provide a consistent way to display colour internet images on computer screens (CRTs).

**ColourMatch RGB**

ColourMatch RGB has a wider colour space than sRGB and was developed to closely simulate CMYK press work. ColourMatch RGB features a lower gamma than that of sRGB. Gamma affects how bright mid-tones appear and so switching to ColourMatch RGB can be a simple way to brighten a photo.

RGB

sRGB

A colour is made up of different quantities of red, green and blue light, given as a ratio such as 88/249/17. These ratios produce different results in different colour spaces, as can be seen in the two green panels (left), which use the RGB and sRGB colour spaces.

In order to have accurate and reliable colour reproduction it is necessary to know how different devices in the design and print production system use colour. Although devices may use colour in different ways, the International Color Consortium has produced a set of profiles to standardise the ways in which devices communicate colour information.

## colour space

Each device used in the graphic design and printing industries produces or reproduces a certain array of colours called a colour space. For example, RGB is the additive primary colour space that computer monitors use and CMYK is the subtractive primary colour space used in the four-colour printing process. Digital cameras, scanners and printers all have colour spaces. Each colour space reproduces a limited amount of colours within the overall spectral colour gamut, in other words the colours that the human eye can perceive.

A digital camera records light as pixels and each pixel records red, green or blue light values. The colour space provides a definition for the numeric value of this combination of colours present in a pixel, with each value representing a different colour. Changing the colour space will change the colour associated to this value, which means that while creating a design or making adjustments to images, it is necessary to be aware of the colour space that is being worked in.

Euroscale Coated/Uncoated

SWOP

## colour profiles

Euroscale Coated is a colour profile that uses specifications designed to produce quality separations using the CMYK process. It was created to define CMYK for offset-printing on glossy paper, with colours generated by mixing the four process colour inks under the following printing conditions: 350 per cent total area of ink coverage, positive plate and bright white-coated stock.

The Euroscale Uncoated profile is a CMYK working space created for use with uncoated stock under the following printing conditions: 260 per cent total area of ink coverage, positive plate and uncoated white offset stock.

SWOP (specifications for web offset publications) is a standard colour profile used to ensure the consistent quality of advertising in publications in North America. Adobe Photoshop uses the SWOP profile as its default for making CMYK colour separations.

# Pantone and spot colours

Graphic designers use spot colours to ensure that a particular colour in a design will print. This may be necessary if the colour is outside the range or gamut of possibilities of the four-colour CMYK printing process, or because there is a pressing need for a specific colour, such as for a corporate logo. Special colours have greater intensity and vibrancy as they print as a solid colour rather than one that is composed of half-tone dots, as the panels below show.

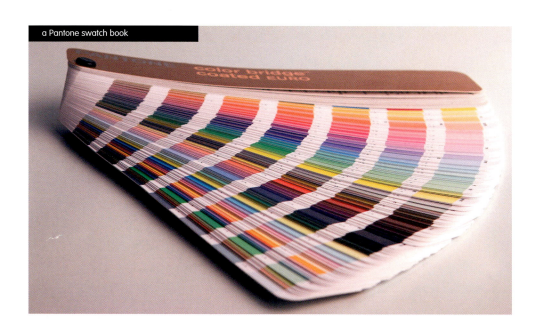

a Pantone swatch book

806 C

| C | M | Y | K |
|---|---|---|---|
| 0 | 50 | 0 | 0 |

806C

CMYK

**spot colours and CMYK**
The far left-hand square is printed as a fluorescent PM 806 spot colour and its nearest CMYK version is printed on the left. The process colour square is much duller than the spot colour version as it is made with half-tone dots of colour, whereas the special colour is applied as a flat colour. The approximation of a CMYK colour to a process colour varies. In this example, the colour conversion uses a 50 per cent magenta and no colour, which does not give the same intensity – it essentially prints as a tint.

## mixing a spot colour

Spot colours are made from various base elements, mixed according to a specific recipe. Spot colour inks can be bought pre-mixed and ready to use or they can be created by mixing the constituent parts. The example, below right, prints with Pantone 8001, a dull silver, but not all printers stock this ink.

However, as it is made from one part Pantone 874 (a bronze) and three parts Pantone 877 (a silver), both of which most printers stock as standard, this special colour can be mixed by the printer if needed.

colour breakdowns

mixing inks

mixed and printed colour

## Pantone systems

The Pantone PMS colour system has developed to include a wide range of different colours, including special solid, hexachrome, metallic and pastel colours.

The Pantone system allocates a unique reference number to each hue and shade to facilitate communication between designers and printers, such as Pantone 806C, the fluorescent spot colour used on this page.

**U** = Uncoated
**C** = Coated
**EC** = Euro coated
**M** = Matte

### Pantone guides explained

**Pantone solid**
A range of solid metallic, pastel and process colours that can be used on different paper stocks and substrates. The fluorescent opposite would be Pantone 806U, 806C or 806M depending upon whether it is to print on matte, coated or uncoated stock.

**Pantone pastels**
A range of flat, solid, but very pale colours. These are different to tints as they print as a solid colour without visible dots. They are available in both coated and uncoated swatches.

**Pantone hexachrome**
A range of six process colours used for hexachrome printing. In addition to the CMYK process colours, the system adds green and orange process colours allowing it to reproduce 90 per cent of the Pantone PMS colours.

**Pantone metallics**
A range of over 300 special colours that give a metallic effect including silver, gold and copper colours. Metallics are available in varnished and unvarnished coated swatches.

# colour correction

Photographs often need colour correction due to an imperfect or inaccurate assessment of the light when shooting.

## basic colour adjustment

Many image manipulation programs feature adjustment tools to make automatic colour adjustments in order to cope with common problems, such as red eye or colour balance problems.

### colour balance

The colour balance command can be used to remove simple colour casts by changing the overall colour mix in an image. This colour correction is performed in relation to the colours within the image. However, by using the techniques explained over the next few pages, designers can exercise more control over colour than these simple commands provide.

Using the Color Balance command, a designer can increase or decrease the amount of a colour in an image by dragging the sliders relating to each colour.

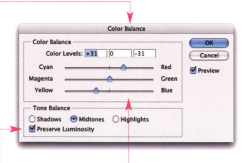

original image / color balanced image

Ticking the Preserve Luminosity box prevents the image's luminosity values changing while the colours are changed, which maintains its tonal balance.

To correct the original image (far left), which has a blue cast, the sliders with blue in them (cyan/red and yellow/blue) have been altered to remove it (left).

### desaturation

Converting an image from the RGB colour space to CMYK will dull its colours because those outside the CMYK gamut suffer distortion (as can be seen below). The lipstick loses its bright red hue while the gold base is less affected. This problem can be avoided using the saturation command. With the image in RGB mode, desaturate it to bring its colours within the CMYK gamut and then convert to CMYK. This will result in an image that is still dull, but more balanced and less distorted.

RGB image / CMYK image

## automated colour features

Various automated correction controls allow the designer to perform simple standard adjustments to an image.

original image

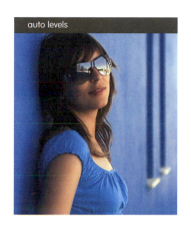
auto levels

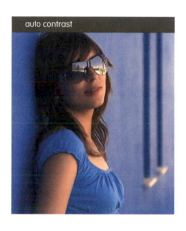
auto contrast

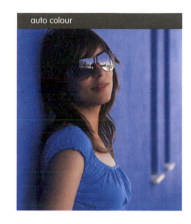
auto colour

This is an image that is to be colour corrected.

In this image the auto colour command neutralises mid-tones on its default setting (using RGB 128 grey), and clips shadow and highlight pixels by 0.5 per cent. The default settings can be changed by the designer.

Auto contrast automatically adjusts the contrast and colour mixture in an RGB image. This command clips shadow and highlight values and maps the remaining lightest and darkest pixels to pure white (level 255) and pure black (level 0). This makes highlights appear lighter and shadows appear darker.

This command adjusts image contrast and colour by neutralising mid-tones (using RGB 128 grey) and clipping shadow and highlight pixels by 0.5 per cent.

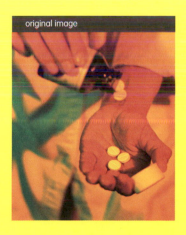
original image

auto levels, contrast and colour

original greyscale image

auto levels and contrast

## correcting in colour

The original image, above left, appears to be suffering from some distracting yellow and orange colour casts. The auto levels, auto contrast and auto colour commands can make a good assumption about how to correct the image based on the mid-tones, highlight and shadow areas, which can provide a designer with a good starting point for colour correction. However, to obtain a good balance (the corrected image still has a red cast), manual adjustment is usually also necessary.

## correcting in greyscale

Although greyscale images contain no colour, the auto contrast and auto level commands can still be used to correct an image by calibrating it to a set of reference parameters. However, fine tuning is best done by eye to obtain a natural-looking result as software programs make assumptions during automatic correction and are unaware of the end result the designer is trying to achieve.

# variations and selective colour

Images can be colour corrected or given colour intervention through the use of the Variations and Selective Color commands in Adobe Photoshop.

### the Variations command

The Variations command allows a designer to adjust image colour balance, contrast and saturation while showing thumbnails of the alternatives. This command is useful when an image does not require precise colour adjustment, but an overall slanting of the colour information in an image.

This simple but effective approach uses a thumbnail of the original image and the adjusted image (current pick) set side by side for direct comparison. The variations of colour options are then set in a circle around the 'current pick' image, allowing a designer to see the different colour possibilities.

**comparable images**
The original image and the changed image are juxtaposed for easy comparison to see the effect the changes are making.

**Mode**
The Mode box allows a designer to select shadows, mid-tones or highlights according to whether adjustments need to be made in the dark, middle or light areas of an image. The Show Clipping option allows a designer to see which colours will be clipped if they exceed their maximum saturation (see below).

**Show Clipping**
The Show Clipping option provides a neon preview of areas in the image that will be clipped and converted to pure white or pure black by the adjustment being made. Clipping does not occur when you adjust mid-tones.

**Current Pick**
This is the image that is being worked on and it is surrounded by potential colour variations, allowing for easy visual comparison.

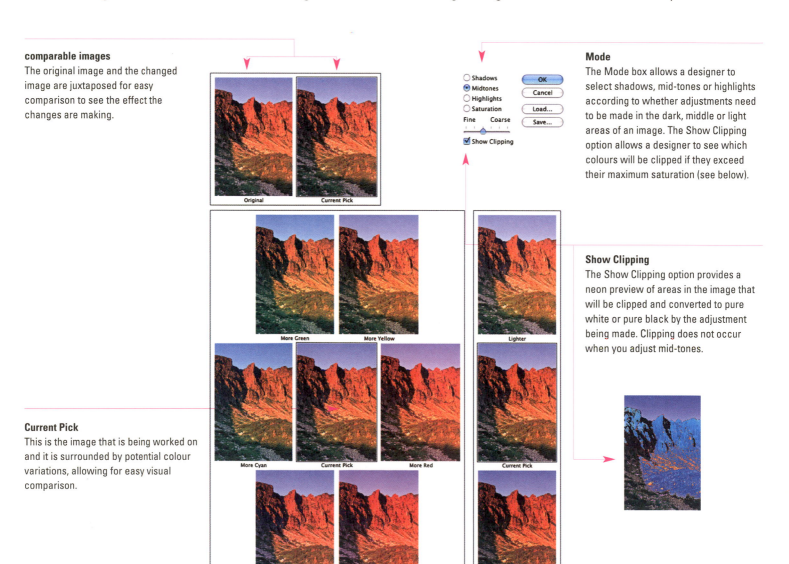

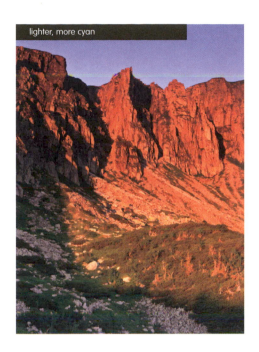

lighter, more cyan

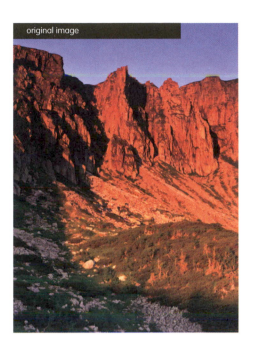

original image

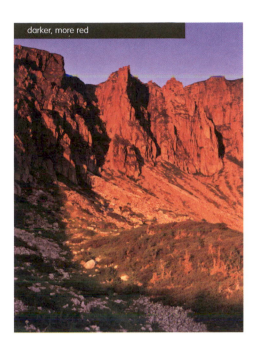

darker, more red

This mountain image has been adjusted and lightened through the addition of cyan. It now has an early morning feel.

The original, unadjusted image.

This image has been made darker and has had more red added to warm it, to create the feeling of sunset.

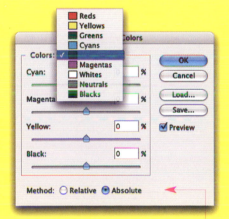

These controls allow a designer to determine whether selective colour is applied relatively or absolutely.

## the Selective Color command

The Selective Color command allows a designer to change the colours within a colour. Selective colour can be applied relatively or absolutely. The relative method changes a colour according to the percentage of the total that it represents. For example, adding 10 per cent to a pixel that is 40 per cent cyan adds 4 per cent to it for a total of 44 per cent cyan. The absolute method applies an absolute value to the change so that in this instance, adding 10 per cent to the 40 per cent cyan changes it to 50 per cent.

The original image above has blue in the sky but little in other areas, so it is possible to alter the blue sky without changing the rest of the image. This is done by changing the values of the subtractive primaries on the blue channel (not the cyan channel). Performing selective colour correction in this way is based on a table showing the amount of each process ink used to create each primary colour. Increasing or decreasing the amount of the process inks in relation to one another means a designer can selectively alter the amount of a process colour in any primary colour without affecting the other primary colours.

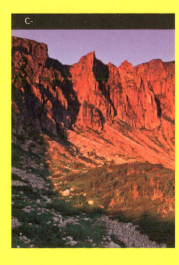

C-

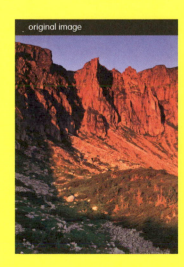

original image

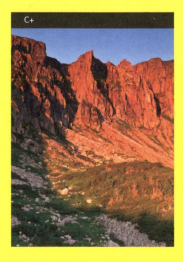

C+

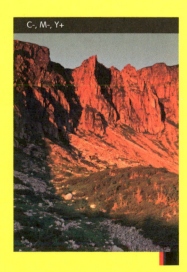

C-, M-, Y+

# removing colour casts

A colour cast exists when the colours in an image are not properly balanced. This typically occurs when a camera's settings are incorrect for the prevailing lighting conditions. A cast can appear across the entire range of pixel values or be limited to the highlight, shadow, or mid-tones of an image.

**Color Balance**
The Color Balance tool allows colour values to be changed between red, green and blue, and cyan, magenta and yellow.

**Tone Balance**
The Tone Balance tool allows a designer to adjust the shadows, highlights or mid-tones. Most colour information is in the mid-tone.

## identifying a colour cast by eye

It may be difficult to detect an imbalance in the colours by eye alone, perhaps due to the surrounding lighting conditions or the colour presentation of the computer screen. However, if you know that an image suffers from a colour cast it can often be altered by using a simple colour balance application. Where you are unsure if there is a colour cast, there are two methods (described opposite) to help identify it.

The Color Balance tool in Photoshop allows a designer to alter shadows, mid-tones and highlights independently of each other and so focuses on specific image areas. In the image below where there is obviously a green cast, removing some of the green in its highlights balances the image. Most colour correction is done in mid-tone areas, as their shadows contain most of the black in an image and their highlights most of the white, meaning that there is normally less to correct here. A photographer will often do this prior to delivering photos to a designer, although this cannot be guaranteed.

image with green colour cast

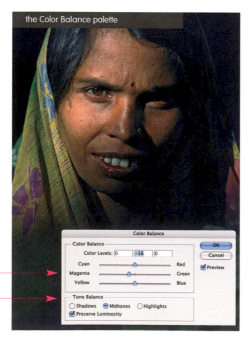
the Color Balance palette

adjusted image

original image with colour cast

red channel

green channel

blue channel

## identifying a cast using channels

Displaying colour channels separately will often reveal colour casts. In the example above left there is clearly an extreme green cast. Looking at the individual colour channels of this image also confirms this. The red and blue channels are clearly stronger than the green channel, indicating that the image suffers from a green cast.

In the same way, the absence of density in the blue channel would reveal a blue cast, and in the red channel, a red cast. Due to the way that channels work, a reduction in the channel value produces an increase in that colour's presence in the image. It is helpful (although this may sound confusing) to think of the channel as a negative – the lighter it is, the more light will flood through, producing a darker image.

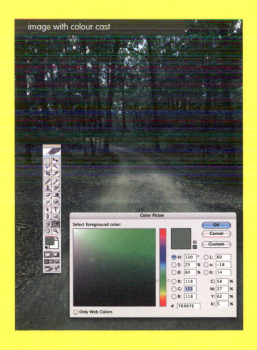

image with colour cast

adjusting curves

corrected image

## identifying a cast using a colour picker

Another method designers use for detecting colour casts is to use a colour picker and select something in the image that they are certain should be colour neutral, such as a sample of a stone on the floor. The colour picker here reveals a distinct green tinge. Using the colour curves, a designer can select that colour channel and alter it until the image colour is adequately corrected.

## using curves

A curve is a graph or line along which each point represents a combination of two variables, such as two different colours. Changing the shape of the graph by adding new points allows these variables to be altered to change the colour in an image. It is possible to adjust either individual channels or the image as a whole.

# colour correction using hue

Hue is the colour reflected or transmitted from an object, so adjusting the hue of an image in Photoshop is a quick and easy way of altering its colour.

### altering colour

Colour correction can be subtle or dramatic, depending on the need of a design. Using the Hue option allows colour alteration without changing the colour saturation, luminance or shadows and highlights of the original image. Put simply, if you want to turn a red apple into a green one, this can be easily done by placing a layer of the colour you want over the original image, rather like a photographer uses a colour gel over the lens.

### limitations

The use of hue to correct colour has its limitations as all the information in the image is subject to the same degree of colour change. This tinting can be avoided by removing sections from the coloured layer. Shown below is the coloured apple layer with the eaten section and stalk removed, meaning the skin will be altered but the flesh and stalk will remain unchanged.

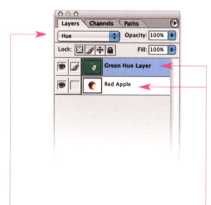

**original image**
This is the original image of a red apple.

**blend option**
Set to Hue, the blend option will alter the colour of the image underneath.

**original image and coloured layer**
The original image is set as the base image and blended with the green hue layer to produce this resulting image.

**hue layer**
This is the hue layer that is blended with the original image to produce the colour-adjusted image.

The sequence below shows how the hue of an image can be changed or corrected through the use of layers. The original image is changed from red to blue and then green by blending a hue layer with the original image, subtly altering the white areas.

Changing the model's hair colour is a more subtle example. A layer matching the shape of the model's face was created in order to allow the designer to make adjustments to the model's hair and face independently of each other.

original image

The original, unaltered image.

'hair' layer

Adding a red layer to the background area will affect the hair only.

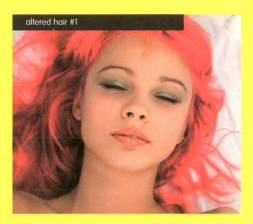

altered hair #1

Applying a red hue layer over the hair alters the colour of the hair only, as the background is white and remains relatively unaltered.

altered hair #2

Adding a grey layer results in the hair becoming a silvery grey colour.

warm skin tones

By adding additional hue layers, image elements can be altered independently. Here, the skin tones are warmed.

cool skin tones

Skin tones can also be cooled.

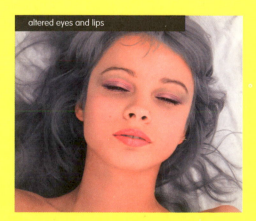

altered eyes and lips

With another adjustment layer, the colour of the eyes and lips can be altered.

lightened

Further adjustments can be made to independent layers or the image as a whole.

contrast adjusted

These adjustments can be undertaken until the desired result is achieved.

# dodge and burn

Dodge and burn effects are used to lighten or darken areas of an image, and are based on techniques traditionally used by photographers to regulate exposure on specific areas of a print.

### dodge
Photographers hold back light when exposing photographic film in order to lighten an area of the print. This is called dodging. Dodging essentially lightens pixels where you paint.

### burn
Photographers increase the exposure to light when exposing photographic film to darken areas. This is called burning. Burning essentially darkens pixels where you paint.

### colour images
When used with colour prints or images, dodging and burning gives a designer the ability to alter highlights, mid-tones (where most colour information is kept) or shadows. Fortunately these techniques are very forgiving so if a bit of background is dodged or burned, it will not be too obvious because these tools alter saturation rather than hue.

By preserving the basic colour information, subtle alterations to the original images using saturation and brightness can be made with ease. The lightest image areas are affected when focusing on highlights, the darkest areas when working on shadows, and mid-tones when working on mid-tones.

The dodge tool is used to make image areas lighter. In the image above, the hair, eyes, parts of the face and arms, and the background surf have been dodged, as well as the pattern on the t-shirt.

This is the original, unaltered image. Dodge and burn can be used to suppress or highlight areas of the image, to compensate, for example, for poor lighting conditions at the shoot stage.

In this image, areas of the face and hair have been burned to make them darker, essentially increasing their contrast with other elements within the image.

## greyscale images

Dodge and burn techniques can also be used with a monotone greyscale image to help accentuate details, as seen in the examples below. The dodged image (top) has more detail in darker areas as it lightens pixels, giving the woman's skin more depth. When the image is burned (bottom), the skin loses detail as pixels are darkened, but more detail is seen in darker areas, such as around the eyes and mouth.

## converted images

Converting images from the RGB to CMYK colour space dulls colours, making them appear washed out. A dab with the sponge tool while in saturation mode can help brighten them again. When working on an image in RGB mode that will subsequently be converted to CMYK, a designer can keep an eye out for colours that are not within the CMYK gamut and use the sponge tool in desaturate mode to bring them into it. The sponge tool in desaturate mode can also be used to tone down background colours, enabling the foreground to stand out more or to give a colourised appearance.

areas dodged

saturated image (bright)

original image

converted image (dull)

areas burned

# creative colour

Colour provides dynamism to a design, elevating certain elements and attracting attention in a way that can illicit an emotional response in the viewer. Creative colour use can achieve this by dramatically changing the appearance of something or someone familiar, as these pages show.

## colour layers

Layers can be used to overlay colour panels on to a base image and these can then be blended in different ways to alter the colour of the original image, while leaving the contrast and detail intact.

### effects on images

The images opposite and below have had a solid yellow panel applied in order to demonstrate how an image's appearance can be changed through blending.

While a yellow panel has been used here, there are millions of colours that could be applied, as well as variations of opacity, thus giving a vast range of possible subtle combinations.

This is the original image to which different effects filters have been applied.

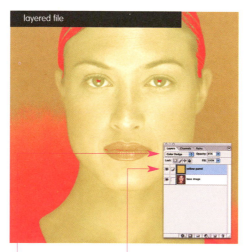

**blend mode**
This control enables a designer to decide how the layer and original image will blend.

**coloured layer panel**
This image blends a colour layer with the original image.

**blending mode selection**
A designer can choose from many different blending modes, such as the difference mode selected here.

colour dodge

The base colour in each channel of this image has been brightened to reflect the blend colour by reducing the contrast. Blending with black produces no change in a colour dodge.

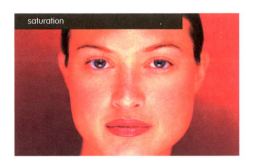

saturation

Saturation produces a colour result based on the luminance and hue of the base colour and saturation of the blend colour. Where there is no saturation in the base image (grey areas), there is no change.

overlay

This effect sees patterns or colours overlaid on to the existing pixels while the base colour highlights and shadows are preserved. The base colour is mixed with the blend colour to reflect the lightness or darkness of the original colour.

multiply

With this effect the colour intensity of the top layer is multiplied with that of the bottom layer to produce darker colours that give more contrast.

vivid light

The blend colour determines if the image is burned or dodged. This lightens lighter than 50 per cent grey or darkens darker than 50 per cent grey.

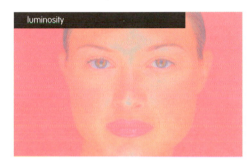

luminosity

Luminosity produces a colour that has the hue and saturation of the base colour and the luminance of the blend colour.

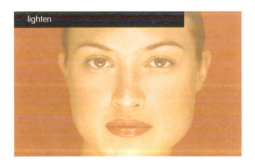

lighten

Here the lightest base or blend colour is selected as the final colour, so darker pixels are replaced with the blend colour while lighter pixels do not change.

hard light

This effect adds highlights to the image if the blend colour is lighter than 50 per cent grey, or adds shadows if it is darker than 50 per cent grey.

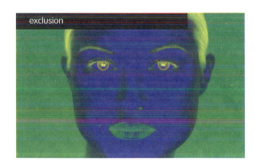

exclusion

The exclusion effect blends the base image with white to invert its colour values, producing a lower contrast version of the Difference effect.

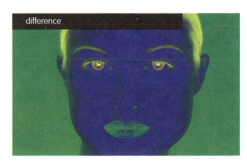

difference

Here the blend colour is subtracted from the base colour or vice versa depending on which has the greater brightness value, while blending with white inverts base colour values.

colour

This effect produces colours with the luminance of the base colour and the hue and saturation of the blend colour, and is used for colouring monochrome and tinting colour images as it preserves grey levels.

hard mix

This effect posterises the base layer pixels through the blend layer and recolours the image by dodging or burning it with a palette of eight colours from the base image.

# multiple images

Various blend modes can also be used to merge separate images in Photoshop. Essentially, this is done by combining the colours of the pixels that comprise each image, using the colour channels that they are formed with.

original image #1

original image #2

In this example, two images of a face have been used: one serves as the base image upon which the other will be overlaid. The processes highlighted here simulate traditional photography practices like a double exposure or the projection of multiple images on to a wall. The advantage here is the degree of control the user has over being able to alter different facets of one image, such as contrast, while leaving the other image unaffected.

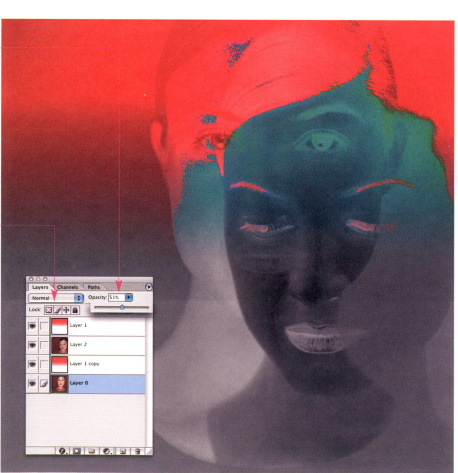

**Opacity**
The Opacity control determines the extent to which one layer shows through to the next. The greater the opacity, the less the image underneath will show through.

**Blend Mode**
A designer can select one of many different methods to specify how the different layers blend.

**multiple layers**
This image is produced with a blend of multiple layers. Each layer can be seen in the command panel.

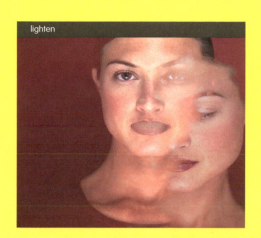

lighten

screen

colour burn

Images can be merged by working with the colour information in each channel in reference to a chosen base colour. In this case, the base or blend colour will be lighter than the final colour and pixels that are darker than this will be replaced. Lighter pixels do not change. The result is a merging of the colours of the images, which become harder to identify on their own.

This process multiplies the inverse of the blend and base colours to produce a lighter colour where the images merge. Applying a black screen produces no colour change, while screening with white produces white. The result is that while the colours merge, both images can still be clearly identified.

This blend uses a chosen colour to colourise the darker pixels of the base image while producing little change to the lighter pixels. This produces a dramatic colour intervention in which both images can be identified.

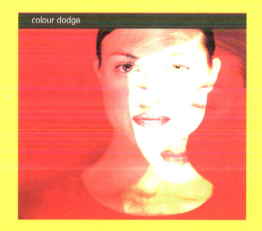

colour dodge

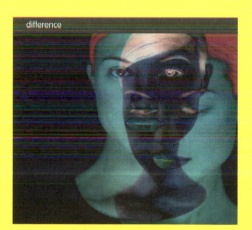

difference

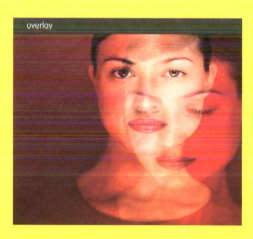

overlay

A colour dodge brightens the base colour so that it is closer to the blend colour, decreases the contrast between the images and helps them to merge so that it is harder to tell them apart.

This process subtracts one colour from the other, depending on which of the base or blend colours has the greater brightness value. Blending the result with white inverts the base colour values, while a black blend produces no change. The result is that where the images meet, a third visual element is created.

This process overlays patterns or colours on the existing pixels while preserving the highlights and shadows of the base colour. In this way the base colour is mixed with the blend colour to reflect the lightness or darkness of the original colour. The result is an image with more intense colours in which both images are identifiable.

# greyscale and toned images

Designers can also make graphic interventions to images in order to make them appear to have been shot in greyscale or toned.

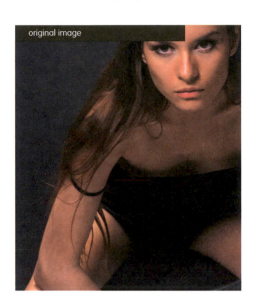
original image

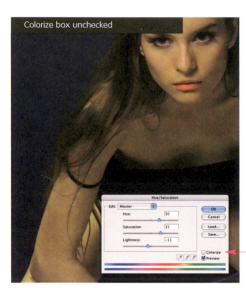
Colorize box unchecked

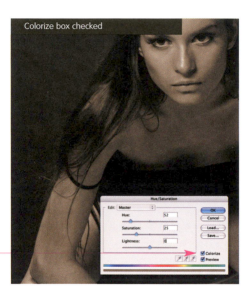
Colorize box checked

### sepia toning images

To create a sepia-toned image, the hue must be changed before working on the light and dark tonal areas. In the Hue/Saturation dialogue box in Photoshop, check the Colorize and Preview boxes and adjust the hue slider to the colour required or enter a value. Then use the saturation slider to determine how much of the hue will be used in the image.

Finally, adjust the highlights and shadows using the levels dialogue box. The three sliders below the chart control the shadows, mid-tones and highlights and can be changed to increase or decrease the level of detail in their respective areas.

### colourising

Colourising is an artistic effect that allows a designer to apply colour detail to a selected area of an image. Checking the Colorize box allows the designer to instantly see the effect of any changes made to hue and saturation. Notice the difference between the centre (Colorize box unchecked) and right (Colorize box checked) images above.

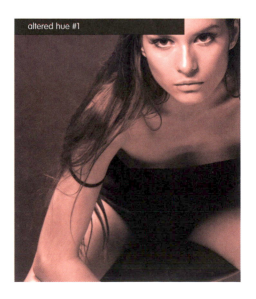
altered hue #1

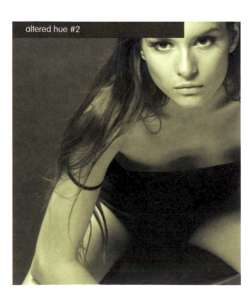
altered hue #2

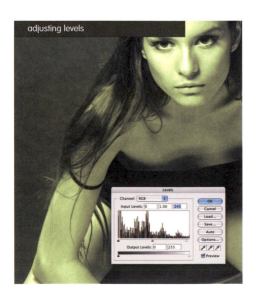
adjusting levels

## converting images to greyscale

Pictured below is an RGB image that can be converted to create a balanced greyscale image such as the one shown below right. The greyscale image contains one channel (grey), made up of information from the three RGB channels that are shown underneath. Alternatively, a greyscale image can be produced from any of the three RGB channels. As the RGB channels represent sensitivity towards different coloured light, each channel has a bias towards the type of light prevalent at different times of the day.

During the early morning, blue light is dominant while red reigns in the evening and green at midday (because neither red or blue are dominant). Externally shot images are generally affected by the sun and so splitting the channels results in three greyscale images with each one being a record of the red, green or blue light. This may give a designer the option, particularly with exterior images, to create an impression of the time of day at which a photograph was shot.

original image

converted to greyscale

blue channel

green channel

red channel

This image relates to the blue channel of the greyscale image, producing a facsimile of the cool morning light.

This image relates to the green channel of the greyscale image, producing a facsimile of the midday light when neither blue nor red are dominant.

This image relates to the red channel of the greyscale image, producing a facsimile of the warm evening light.

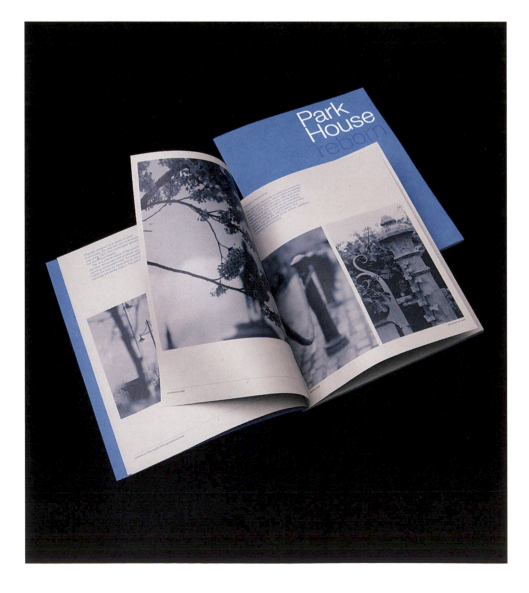

### Environment Agency (above)

These two spreads are taken from an annual report created by design studio, Thirteen, for the UK Environmental Agency. Duotone images are used to provide an element of standardisation and consistency to the publication. The duotones contrast strongly with the white type, which is reversed out of blocks of solid colour to arrest the attention of the reader and show off the information they contain.

### Park House (left)

This is a brochure created by Third Eye Design for the Park House property development in central London. It features the use of a primary blue colour on the cover, from which the title is reversed out and the subtitle is surprinted. The images within the brochure use the same blue in a duotone with black that standardises the images and creates a narrative of connection that builds over the successive pages of the publication.

### Maticevski (facing page)

This poster, created by 3 Deep Design, features the use of four-colour black to produce a strong, impacting colour that is brimming with emotive power. A four-colour black uses the cyan, magenta and yellow process colours as a shiner to intensify the final black produced.

MATICEVSKI

# multi-tones

Duotones, tritones and quadtones are tonal images produced from a monotone original with the use of two-, three- or four-colour tones, normally offset against a black base tone.

### monotone images

Any multi-tone image begins as a monotone image, such as this one of the Coliseum in Rome, Italy. If an image is not already a monotone it needs to be converted into one before it can be worked upon in Photoshop.

original image

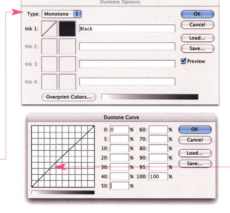

monotone image

**type**

The designer chooses whether the resulting image will be mono-, duo-, tri- or quadtone using one, two, three or four colours respectively.

**Duotone Curve**

Each colour in the multi-tone has a curve that can be altered to change its intensity.

### duotone images

A duotone image is made of two colours, such as the black and yellow shown below. There needs to be a balanced curve to produce a balanced duotone because if the curve is flattened and pushed to the top it will produce a flooded colour, as shown below right.

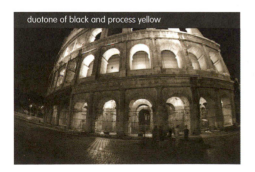
duotone of black and process yellow

duotone with full process yellow

**preset values**

Preset values can be loaded into the software to remove the guesswork from obtaining good contrast, although trial and error, and experimentation can produce effective results.

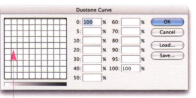

**altering Duotone Curves**

Duotone Curves can be altered to produce subtle or dramatic results. In the examples above, the yellow has been set to run full, flooding the base of the image with colour.

## tritone images

Adding a third colour to a tonal image creates a tritone. The examples below were created using the preset values for the colour curves. For example, the middle image simulates a sepia tone and uses magenta, yellow and black, while the image on the right has added depth and colour as a result of using certain special colours.

If a multitone image is created using Pantone special colours but is to be printed in CMYK, the image colour information needs to be converted to the CMYK colour space once it is complete. This will simulate the Pantone colours in the CMYK colour space. If a special colour is to be used in printing, this can be used in the multi-tone to give a richer colour effect.

warm grey preset tritone

sepia preset tritone

Pantone preset tritone

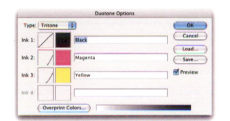

## quadtone images

Adding a fourth colour creates a quadtone. As with tritones, preset values can be used to create specific effects. The middle image below uses all three subtractive primary colours. Adding a fourth colour creates a quadtone. As with tritones, preset values can be used to create specific effects. The middle image uses all four process colours to produce a rich black.

quadtone image

warm process preset quadtone

Pantone preset quadtone

# colour half-tones

The four-colour printing process produces colour images from different sized half-tone dots of cyan, magenta, yellow and black ink, which combine to fool the eye into seeing a continuous-toned image.

original image

colour half-tone

### using half-tones

Colour printing uses separate plates that contain half-tone dots for different printing inks. A designer can manipulate these dots in order to change the appearance of the printed image. Pictured above is an original image, reproduced in the usual way as a continuous-toned image.

Printed here is a graphic interpretation of the same image, but this time using larger half-tone dots to emphasise the fact that it is not actually a continuous tone, but is made up of dots. As can be seen opposite, the composition of these dots is dependent on the mode of the original image – CMYK or RGB.

original image

quick mask

colour half-tone

bordered image

### using half-tones as borders

Half-tone dots can be harnessed to produce different graphic effects such as a creative border on the altered image. Here, a quick mask was applied (by pressing 'q' in Photoshop) and turned into a colour half-tone using the colour half-tone filter. Notice that the mask is smaller than the image. This is because any filtering will sample the image.

Select the dot radius required (from very small, fine dots to the bolder interventions used here) and apply. Remove the mask and delete the border area and any irregular or deformed dots around the perimeter to give a creative image frame.

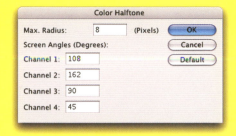

original image

colour half-tone in RGB mode
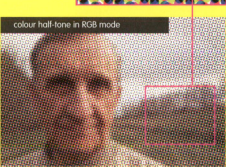

colour half-tone in CMYK mode
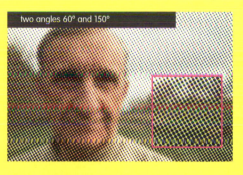

## CMYK, RGB and greyscale

The half-tone dots of each colour plate interact to create the impression of a continuous tone because they are aligned at different screen angles. These angles vary depending upon the colour mode or colour space used. RGB dots replicate those of a computer screen while CMYK dots replicate those used in printing. Any changes to the half-tone dots therefore need to be made in the different colour channels of the colour space used.

The radius of the dots (their size) and the angles of each colour can be altered independently in the dialogue box (top left). For greyscale images, only channel 1 should be used. For RGB images, channels 1, 2, and 3, which correspond to the red, green and blue channels are used, and for CMYK images, all four channels, corresponding to the cyan, magenta, yellow, and black channels are used.

all angles 60°
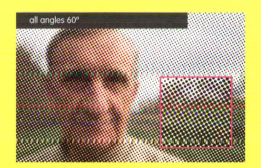

two angles 60° and 150°
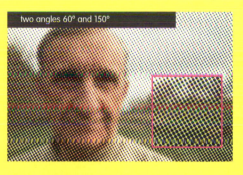

angles set at 0°, 60° and 120°
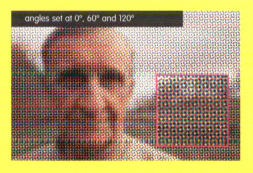

original greyscale image

greyscale half-tone
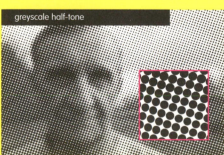

change of dot size and angle
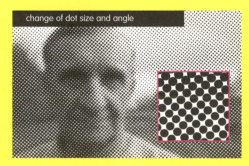

## altering screen angles

When the screen angles are not set correctly they interfere and create moiré patterns that disrupt the impression of a continuous tone.

Different effects and patterns can be achieved by changing the screen angles (the angle of the dot from the horizontal) relating to the different printing inks. This can be done intentionally to add graphic effect, but be careful not to add a moiré.

# colour in print

Before sending a design to print a designer can use a range of methods to ensure that the colours used will appear as intended.

### getting the basics right

When work is sent to print, it is unlikely that there will be further opportunities to rectify mistakes.

For this reason, it is vital that checks are carried out on some of the most basic elements.

#### preparing colour for print

On completion, the designer must carry out a number of pre-press checks to ensure clear communication between designer, client and printer. This is vitally important if the client is to end up with the work that they have been expecting.

A designer must also review certain elements that may pose printing problems. The checklist below shows some common colour pitfalls when sending files to print. Innovative use of print processes that can help a designer get around the restrictions of a limited budget will also be discussed.

#### printed pages and panels

Printed pages (or PP) refers to the actual number of pages printed and not the number of sheets printed on. For example, a booklet made from four sheets with print on every side will have eight printed pages once folded. The key is to remember that one sheet printed double-sided is equal to two printed pages. The same rule of thumb applies to the use of panels, which is simply another way of folding a printed sheet.

**paper**
This dialogue box indicates paper not white, meaning that the item will not be printed but will appear as the same colour as the printing stock.

**before sending a file to print:**

1 Delete all unused colours.

2 Ensure all that you want to print in black is actually in black, not in registration, as registration will print in all plates.

3 Ensure all that should be in registration is in registration, and not in black, as black will only print on the black plate.

4 Ensure all spot colours are accounted for. If the job is printing with a special colour, all is well; if the job is printing CMYK only, then turn all spot colours to CMYK.

5 Ensure all images are converted to CMYK and not RGB. This includes logos, maps, additional icons, for example. In certain circumstances the printer may prefer the files to be left in RGB for them to convert themselves to match a specific profile, but you can't assume this.

6 Ensure you are clear that your colour-fall matches the printer's expectations. If the printer is expecting a four-colour job then supplying a file with special spot colours will cause confusion.

7 Ensure your imported swatches are of the right value, if the job is being printed on uncoated, then set any spot colours as uncoated, and not coated or unspecified.

## London Underground map (left)

Created in the 1930s, Harry Beck's original map of the London Underground features different colours to form a simple and easy-to-follow visual guide to the different train lines. Beck's design was successful because he focused on the approximate relationship of the stations to each other, rather than the distance between them. By discarding scale, Beck was able to construct a highly functional visual representation of the network that bears only a general relation to physical geography.

## River Island (below left)

Pictured here is a brochure created by Third Eye Design for fashion retailer River Island. The brochure is a sheet printed on both sides with six parallel folds to create 14 pages or panels that nest within each other when folded. The use of such formats and folding techniques gives a designer the opportunity to reduce print costs. For example, this job could print four back one, in other words four colours on one side and a single colour on the other, or four back two.

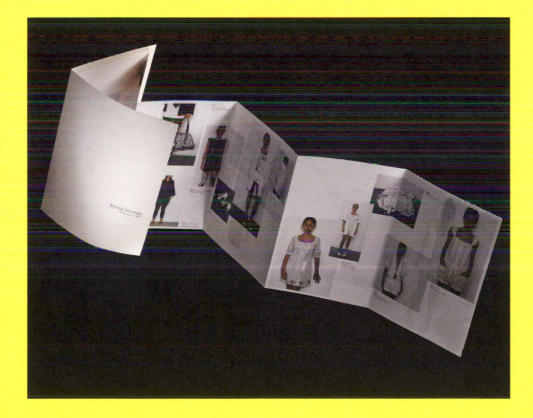

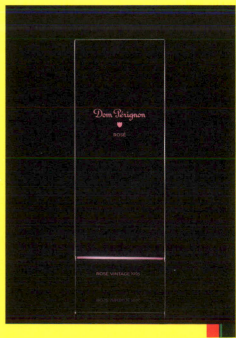

## Dom Pérignon (right)

This packaging design by Research Studios for Dom Pérignon champagne is a good example of the saying 'less is more'. A sense of luxury and value is conveyed through the use of a single colour on a high-quality black stock. Black is often associated with power and exclusivity, and this combines in the minimalist design with a luxurious amount of space to create positive associations to the product. This design could have been printed black on white with the design reversed out, but here it was screen-printed in white on a black stock to provide total control over the quality of the black.

# tints and mixing colours

Process and special colours can be combined using tints and overprinting to produce many different colour effects.

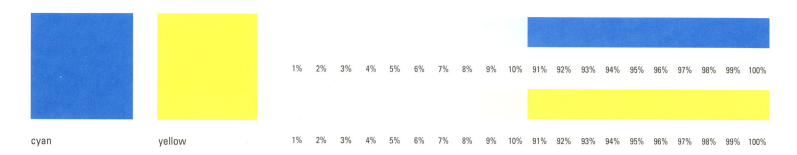

cyan  yellow

1% 2% 3% 4% 5% 6% 7% 8% 9% 10% 91% 92% 93% 94% 95% 96% 97% 98% 99% 100%

1% 2% 3% 4% 5% 6% 7% 8% 9% 10% 91% 92% 93% 94% 95% 96% 97% 98% 99% 100%

## tints

The three trichromatic process colours (cyan, magenta and yellow) can be printed in increments of ten per cent to produce 1,330 tints (or over 15,000 if black is included as well). However, tints below ten per cent and above 90 per cent may not print accurately due to the effect of dot gain.

To see how tints will appear on the final job, a tint bar can be printed on the trim edge of the wet proof. Depending on how they print, adjustments can then be made prior to final printing. This is the only way to see if or how low tints will register because wet proofs use the actual press (pressure, paper, ink) and printing conditions of the final job.

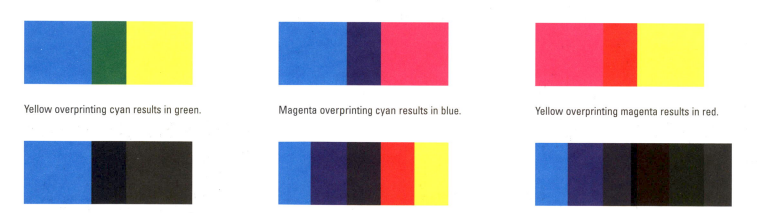

Yellow overprinting cyan results in green.

Magenta overprinting cyan results in blue.

Yellow overprinting magenta results in red.

Black overprinting cyan produces a richer black. Enriching a black in this way is called a shiner.

Three colours overprinting produces a muddy black.

All four process colours overprinting.

## overprinting

Overprinting is where one ink overprints another so that they mix to create different colours. As colour theory dictates, overprinting pairs of the three trichromatic subtractive primary process colours produces the additive primary colours, as shown above. Different blacks can also be achieved with overprinting.

To overprint effectively, a designer needs to bear in mind the order in which the process colours print (see pages 142–143). If printing in the order cyan, magenta, yellow and black, the yellow obviously cannot overprint cyan, for example. Overprinting can produce creative effects when used with graphics and images, and is looked at in more detail on page 120.

cyan

yellow

50% cyan
50% yellow

80% cyan
20% yellow

30% cyan
30% yellow

80% cyan
80% yellow

50% cyan
50% magenta
20% yellow

20% cyan
20% magenta
70% yellow

50% cyan
50% magenta
50% yellow

50% cyan
50% magenta
50% yellow
50% black

20% cyan
20% magenta
20% yellow
20% black

50% cyan
20% magenta
60% yellow
30% black

## multi-ink

Tints of two or more process colours can be combined to create new colour combinations using the multi-ink function. A designer can select different colours and tint levels, such as those above, although the combined colour gets duller as more colours are selected. The percentages of the individual colours used can be combined to create a wide variety of potential colours.

Pantone CMYK breakdowns work in the same way as they produce colours from percentages of the process colours. Working with two colours may seem restrictive, but colour mixing presents options to increase the colour palette. Printing process colour pairs provides the option of using one of the additive RGB primaries, as shown on the opposite page.

## model

The model menu in QuarkXPress's Edit Colour panel presents different options for colour editing, such as multi-ink. While designers are familiar with models such as Pantone, multi-ink offers benefits when printing with a restricted colour gamut, or when attempting to make definite colours with CMYK. The colour swatch indicated shows the colour created by the mix, in this case a light green.

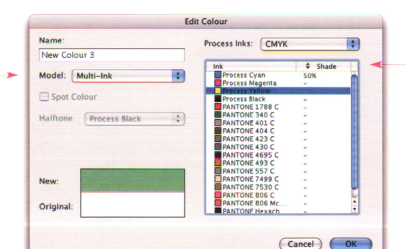

## shade

Shade refers to the tint percentage of the colour that will be used. In this example, a 50 per cent process yellow is highlighted, and this will be combined with a 50 per cent tint of cyan to produce a new colour.

## a note about percentages

As each CMYK ink can be applied with a value ranging from 0 to 100 per cent, a colour is therefore expressed as the percentages of each ink. The total of these values should not exceed 240 because this will result in a muddy colour, as shown right. The middle panel shows a well balanced colour while the right-hand panel shows how it is difficult to achieve a very light tint because the colours 'drop off', or fail to register when printing.

65% cyan
65% magenta
65% yellow
65% black

30% cyan
60% magenta
40% yellow
10% black

2% cyan
2% magenta
2% yellow
2% black

## tint charts

The chart below shows the 121 tint variations that can be obtained when cyan and black are combined in ten per cent increments. Over 1,000 different tints can be produced by combining the cyan, magenta and yellow process colours together in a similar way as shown in the swatches opposite, with even more variations possible if black is added as well. Over 300 tints can be obtained by combining one of the process colours with black and the same amount again by using single tints of these colours.

These swatches enable a designer to obtain a reasonable idea of the colour that will result when combining tints of the different process colours. However, the accuracy of these representations depends upon colour control during the printing process, the press used and the stock that a design is printed upon.

Using tints allows a designer to increase the range of colour possibilities available when the budget for a job is insufficient to cover the cost of four-colour printing. Instead of being limited to the use of two single colours, for example, a designer still has a varied, although limited, colour palette available.

As tints are produced using half-tone dots, very light tints such as those of less than ten per cent may not reproduce well, which is why the rule of thumb minimum is ten per cent.

**four-colour tints of black and cyan**

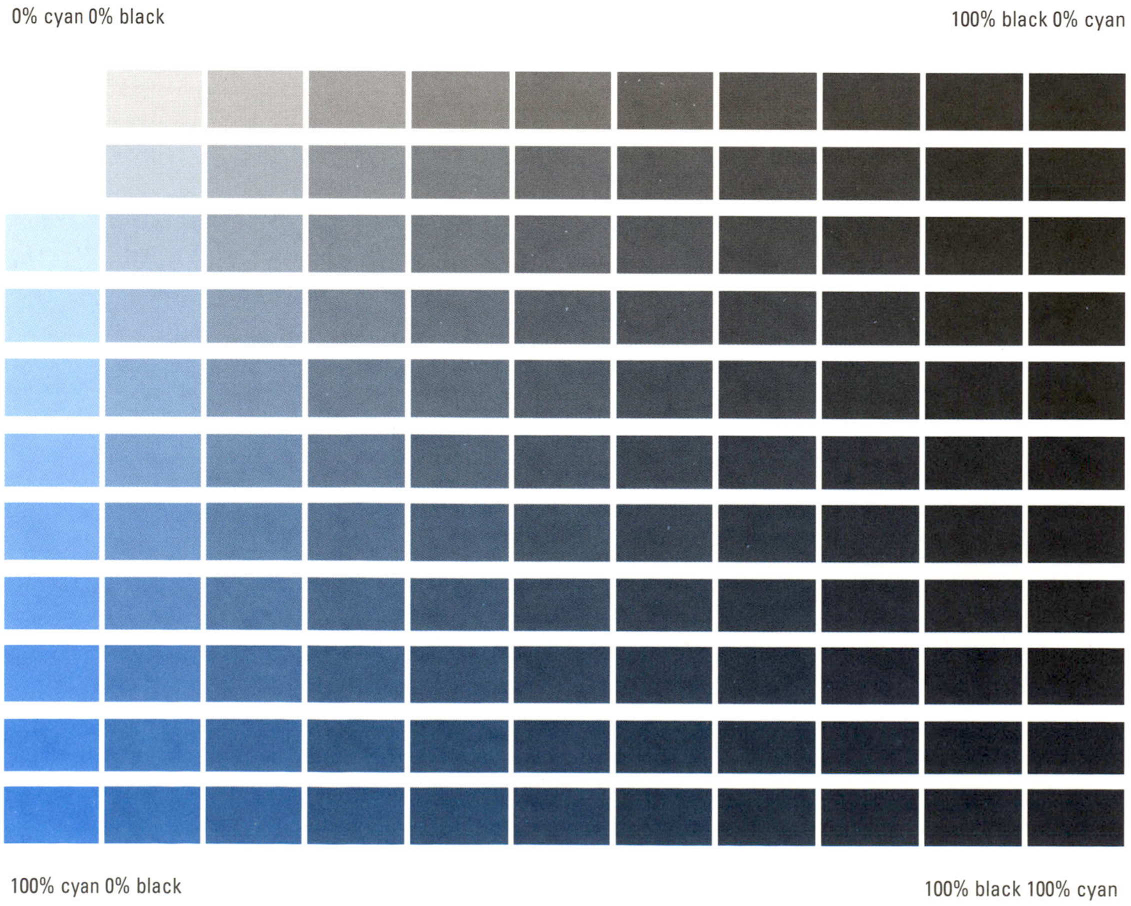

0% cyan 0% black                    100% black 0% cyan

100% cyan 0% black                  100% black 100% cyan

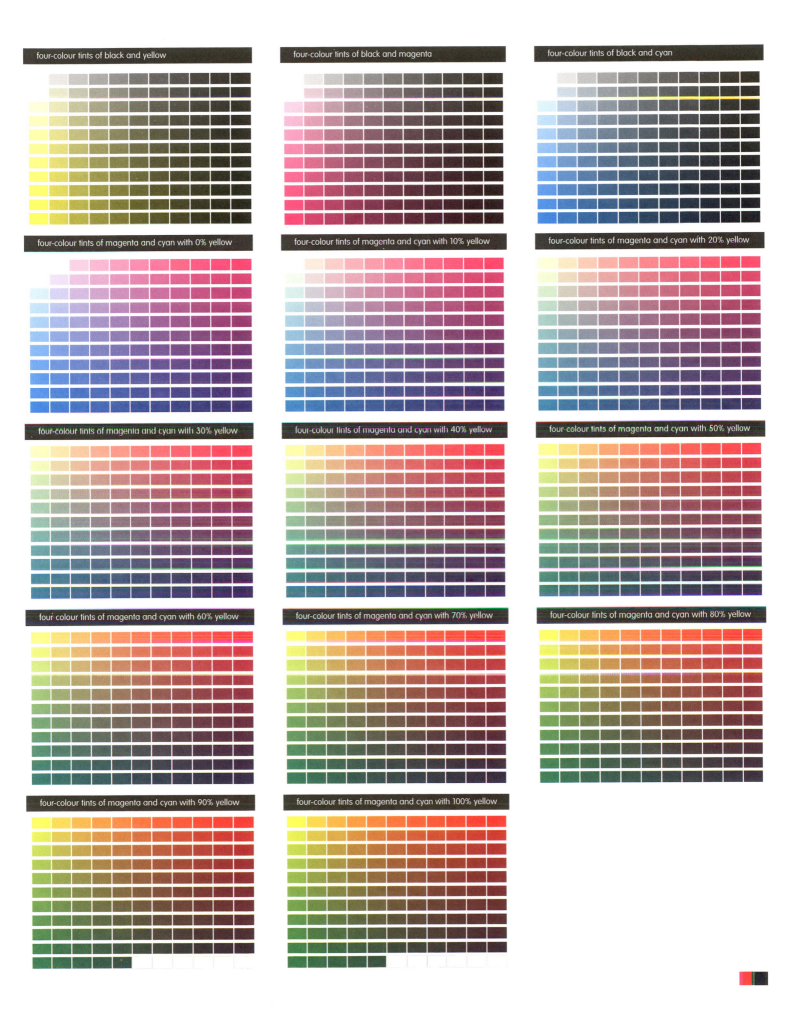

four-colour tints of black and yellow

four-colour tints of black and magenta

four-colour tints of black and cyan

four-colour tints of magenta and cyan with 0% yellow

four-colour tints of magenta and cyan with 10% yellow

four-colour tints of magenta and cyan with 20% yellow

four-colour tints of magenta and cyan with 30% yellow

four-colour tints of magenta and cyan with 40% yellow

four-colour tints of magenta and cyan with 50% yellow

four-colour tints of magenta and cyan with 60% yellow

four-colour tints of magenta and cyan with 70% yellow

four-colour tints of magenta and cyan with 80% yellow

four-colour tints of magenta and cyan with 90% yellow

four-colour tints of magenta and cyan with 100% yellow

# colour on screen

On-screen colour can be controlled using web-safe colours that ensure consistent colour reproduction regardless of the screen a web page is being viewed upon.

## web-safe colours

Web-safe colours are a group of 216 colours, considered to be safe for use in the design of web pages. This palette came into being when computer monitors were only able to display 256 colours and were chosen to match the colour palettes of leading web browsers of the time. The web-safe colour palette allows for the production of six shades of red, green and blue. This palette has the highest number of distinct colours, within which each colour can be distinguished individually.

### generating colours in HTML (hex triplet)

Colours are represented in HTML using a hex triplet, which is a six-digit, three-byte hexadecimal number. Each byte refers to either red, green or blue (in that order) with a range of 00 to FF (hexadecimal notation) or 0 to 255 (decimal notation).

For example, producing all three colours at full value results in white, while producing all colours at a level of zero results in black. On-screen colours behave in this way due to their values of light. When all are on they produce white, all off and they produce black, and variants in between produce colours.

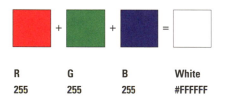

| R | G | B | White |
|---|---|---|---|
| 255 | 255 | 255 | #FFFFFF |

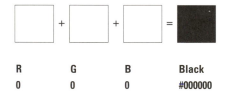

| R | G | B | Black |
|---|---|---|---|
| 0 | 0 | 0 | #000000 |

| R | G | B | Yellow |
|---|---|---|---|
| 255 | 255 | 0 | #FFFF00 |

### HTML colour names

The HTML colour palette includes 16 named colours that are pictured below together with their hex triplet notations. This provides a very basic colour palette that can be recognised

and used by any web browser on any screen. These colours may be specified by name in some applications, and their names are case-independent.

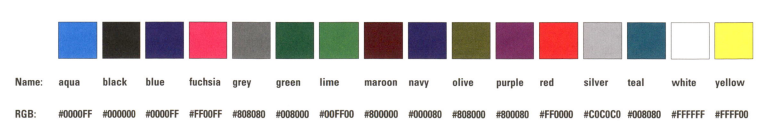

| Name: | aqua | black | blue | fuchsia | grey | green | lime | maroon | navy | olive | purple | red | silver | teal | white | yellow |
|---|---|---|---|---|---|---|---|---|---|---|---|---|---|---|---|---|
| RGB: | #0000FF | #000000 | #0000FF | #FF00FF | #808080 | #008000 | #00FF00 | #800000 | #000080 | #808000 | #800080 | #FF0000 | #C0C0C0 | #008080 | #FFFFFF | #FFFF00 |

## red colours

| IndianRed | CD 5C 5C | 205 92 92 |
|---|---|---|
| LightCoral | F0 80 80 | 240 128 128 |
| Salmon | FA 80 72 | 250 128 114 |
| DarkSalmon | E9 96 7A | 233 150 122 |
| LightSalmon | FF A0 7A | 255 160 122 |
| Crimson | DC 14 3C | 220 20 60 |
| Red | FF 00 00 | 255 0 0 |
| FireBrick | B2 22 22 | 178 34 34 |
| DarkRed | 8B 00 00 | 139 0 0 |

## pink colours

| Pink | FF C0 CB | 255 192 203 |
|---|---|---|
| LightPink | FF B6 C1 | 255 182 193 |
| HotPink | FF 69 B4 | 255 105 180 |
| DeepPink | FF 14 93 | 255 20 147 |
| MediumVioletRed | C7 15 85 | 199 21 133 |
| PaleVioletRed | DB 70 93 | 219 112 147 |

## orange colours

| LightSalmon | FF A0 7A | 255 160 122 |
|---|---|---|
| Coral | FF 7F 50 | 255 127 80 |
| Tomato | FF 63 47 | 255 99 71 |
| OrangeRed | FF 45 00 | 255 69 0 |
| DarkOrange | FF 8C 00 | 255 140 0 |
| Orange | FF A5 00 | 255 165 0 |

## yellow colours

| Gold | FF D7 00 | 255 215 0 |
|---|---|---|
| Yellow | FF FF 00 | 255 255 0 |
| LightYellow | FF FF E0 | 255 255 224 |
| LemonChiffon | FF FA CD | 255 250 205 |
| LightGoldenrodYellow | FA FA D2 | 250 250 210 |
| PapayaWhip | FF EF D5 | 255 239 213 |
| Moccasin | FF E4 B5 | 255 228 181 |
| PeachPuff | FF DA B9 | 255 218 185 |
| PaleGoldenrod | EE E8 AA | 238 232 170 |
| Khaki | F0 E6 8C | 240 230 140 |
| DarkKhaki | BD B7 6B | 189 183 107 |

## purple colours

| Lavender | E6 E6 FA | 230 230 250 |
|---|---|---|
| Thistle | D8 BF D8 | 216 191 216 |
| Plum | DD A0 DD | 221 160 221 |
| Violet | EE 82 EE | 238 130 238 |
| Orchid | DA 70 D6 | 218 112 214 |
| Fuchsia | FF 00 FF | 255 0 255 |
| Magenta | FF 00 FF | 255 0 255 |
| MediumOrchid | BA 55 D3 | 186 85 211 |
| MediumPurple | 93 70 DB | 147 112 219 |
| BlueViolet | 8A 2B E2 | 138 43 226 |
| DarkViolet | 94 00 D3 | 148 0 211 |
| DarkOrchid | 99 32 CC | 153 50 204 |
| DarkMagenta | 8B 00 8B | 139 0 139 |
| Purple | 80 00 80 | 128 0 128 |
| Indigo | 4B 00 82 | 75 0 130 |
| SlateBlue | 6A 5A CD | 106 90 205 |
| DarkSlateBlue | 48 3D 8B | 72 61 139 |

## green colours

| GreenYellow | AD FF 2F | 173 255 47 |
|---|---|---|
| Chartreuse | 7F FF 00 | 127 255 0 |
| LawnGreen | 7C FC 00 | 124 252 0 |
| Lime | 00 FF 00 | 0 255 0 |
| LimeGreen | 32 CD 32 | 50 205 50 |
| PaleGreen | 98 FB 98 | 152 251 152 |
| LightGreen | 90 EE 90 | 144 238 144 |
| MediumSpringGreen | 00 FA 9A | 0 250 154 |
| SpringGreen | 00 FF 7F | 0 255 127 |
| MediumSeaGreen | 3C B3 71 | 60 179 113 |
| SeaGreen | 2E 8B 57 | 46 139 87 |
| ForestGreen | 22 8B 22 | 34 139 34 |
| Green | 00 80 00 | 0 128 0 |
| DarkGreen | 00 64 00 | 0 100 0 |
| YellowGreen | 9A CD 32 | 154 205 50 |
| OliveDrab | 6B 8E 23 | 107 142 35 |
| Olive | 80 80 00 | 128 128 0 |
| DarkOliveGreen | 55 6B 2F | 85 107 47 |
| MediumAquamarine | 66 CD AA | 102 205 170 |
| DarkSeaGreen | 8F BC 8F | 143 188 143 |
| LightSeaGreen | 20 B2 AA | 32 178 170 |
| DarkCyan | 00 8B 8B | 0 139 139 |
| Teal | 00 80 80 | 0 128 128 |

## blue colours

| Aqua | 00 FF FF | 0 255 255 |
|---|---|---|
| Cyan | 00 FF FF | 0 255 255 |
| LightCyan | E0 FF FF | 224 255 255 |
| PaleTurquoise | AF EE EE | 175 238 238 |
| Aquamarine | 7F FF D4 | 127 255 212 |
| Turquoise | 40 E0 D0 | 64 224 208 |
| MediumTurquoise | 48 D1 CC | 72 209 204 |
| DarkTurquoise | 00 CE D1 | 0 206 209 |
| CadetBlue | 5F 9E A0 | 95 158 160 |
| SteelBlue | 46 82 B4 | 70 130 180 |
| LightSteelBlue | B0 C4 DE | 176 196 222 |
| PowderBlue | B0 E0 E6 | 176 224 230 |
| LightBlue | AD D8 E6 | 173 216 230 |
| SkyBlue | 87 CE EB | 135 206 235 |
| LightSkyBlue | 87 CE FA | 135 206 250 |
| DeepSkyBlue | 00 BF FF | 0 191 255 |
| DodgerBlue | 1E 90 FF | 30 144 255 |
| CornflowerBlue | 64 95 ED | 100 149 237 |
| MediumSlateBlue | 7B 68 EE | 123 104 238 |
| RoyalBlue | 41 69 E1 | 65 105 225 |
| Blue | 00 00 FF | 0 0 255 |
| MediumBlue | 00 00 CD | 0 0 205 |
| DarkBlue | 00 00 8B | 0 0 139 |
| Navy | 00 00 80 | 0 0 128 |
| MidnightBlue | 19 19 70 | 25 25 112 |

## brown colours

| Cornsilk | FF F8 DC | 255 248 220 |
|---|---|---|
| BlanchedAlmond | FF EB CD | 255 235 205 |
| Bisque | FF E4 C4 | 255 228 196 |
| NavajoWhite | FF DE AD | 255 222 173 |
| Wheat | F5 DE B3 | 245 222 179 |
| BurlyWood | DE B8 87 | 222 184 135 |
| Tan | D2 B4 8C | 210 180 140 |
| RosyBrown | BC 8F 8F | 188 143 143 |
| SandyBrown | F4 A4 60 | 244 164 96 |
| Goldenrod | DA A5 20 | 218 165 32 |
| DarkGoldenrod | B8 86 0B | 184 134 11 |
| Peru | CD 85 3F | 205 133 63 |
| Chocolate | D2 69 1E | 210 105 30 |
| SaddleBrown | 8B 45 13 | 139 69 19 |
| Sienna | A0 52 2D | 160 82 45 |
| Brown | A5 2A 2A | 165 42 42 |
| Maroon | 80 00 00 | 128 0 0 |

## white colours

| White | FF FF FF | 255 255 255 |
|---|---|---|
| Snow | FF FA FA | 255 250 250 |
| Honeydew | F0 FF F0 | 240 255 240 |
| MintCream | F5 FF FA | 245 255 250 |
| Azure | F0 FF FF | 240 255 255 |
| AliceBlue | F0 F8 FF | 240 248 255 |
| GhostWhite | F8 F8 FF | 248 248 255 |
| WhiteSmoke | F5 F5 F5 | 245 245 245 |
| Seashell | FF F5 EE | 255 245 238 |
| Beige | F5 F5 DC | 245 245 220 |
| OldLace | FD F5 E6 | 253 245 230 |
| FloralWhite | FF FA F0 | 255 250 240 |
| Ivory | FF FF F0 | 255 255 240 |
| AntiqueWhite | FA EB D7 | 250 235 215 |
| Linen | FA F0 E6 | 250 240 230 |
| LavenderBlush | FF F0 F5 | 255 240 245 |
| MistyRose | FF E4 E1 | 255 228 225 |

## grey colours

| Gainsboro | DC DC DC | 220 220 220 |
|---|---|---|
| LightGrey | D3 D3 D3 | 211 211 211 |
| Silver | C0 C0 C0 | 192 192 192 |
| DarkGrey | A9 A9 A9 | 169 169 169 |
| Grey | 80 80 80 | 128 128 128 |
| DimGrey | 69 69 69 | 105 105 105 |
| LightSlateGrey | 77 88 99 | 119 136 153 |
| SlateGrey | 70 80 90 | 112 128 144 |
| DarkSlateGrey | 2F 4F 4F | 47 79 79 |
| Black | 00 00 00 | 0 0 0 |

### X11 colour names

Most modern web browsers support a wider range of colour names from the X11 networking and display protocol list. This features 140 names that are presented above. These can be used either by name or their RGB hex triplet value.

## chapter four

# pre-press

Pre-press encompasses a range of different processes through which the raw materials for the visual elements of a print job are created and brought together in the final design and prepared for the printing process.

This chapter will discuss aspects such as scanning images, resolution, file formats, page imposition, ink-trapping and proofing, in addition to many other methods that are used to produce a printed product. The pre-press stage is the time at which any aspects that may cause printing problems later on must be addressed.

**'Situations' (facing page)**
This publication, created by Thirteen, features a faint, exposed baseline grid on to which the text and image elements have been placed. The careful selection of colours creates a hierarchy on the front cover that refers to the contents.

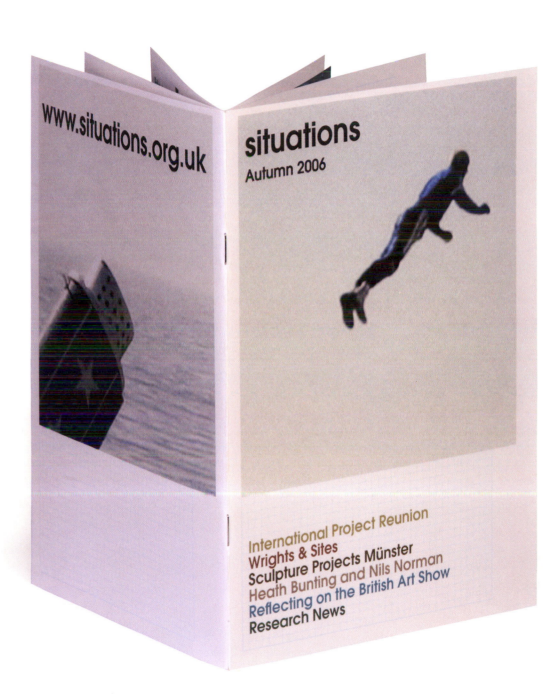

# resolution

The resolution of a digital image is determined by the amount of information it has. Images containing more information have a higher resolution.

## resolution and pixel depth

Resolution is also determined by pixel depth: the number of bits available to generate a colour for each pixel. Greater bit depth means that more colours are available and more accurate colour reproduction is possible in the digital image. The examples below look at this in more detail.

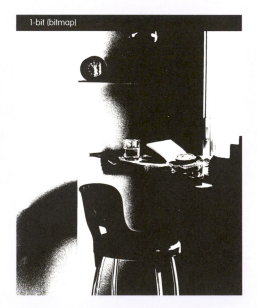

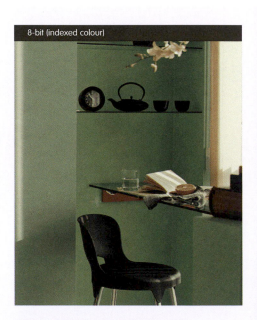

1-bit pixel depth means that an image has either black or white pixels and so no continuous tones are possible. For this reason, 1-bit pixel depth is used for line art images rather than photos.

8-bit pixel depth means it is possible to reproduce 256 shades of grey, that is 8 to the power of two possible values. 8-bit pixel depth allows the reproduction of the continuous tones of a photograph as shown above.

8-bit pixel depth can also reproduce a palette of 256 colours. This is used for basic screen reproduction and was the system used by older computer monitors. While 8-bit colour can reproduce continuous tones, its limited colour range results in washed-out looking images, such as the one above, and so this is best used with GIF images for online use. The term 8-bit is, confusingly, also used to describe 24-bit RGB images (see facing page).

**A**

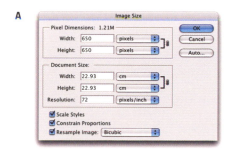

**B**

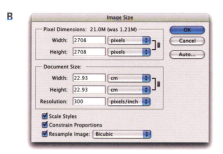

**C**

Understanding the relationship between the pixel dimension of an image and its print resolution allows the production of high-quality print images. The amount of detail an image contains depends on its pixel dimensions and image resolution controls how much space pixels are printed over. In this way, a designer can modify image resolution without changing its pixel data. All that changes is the image print size. Maintaining the same output dimensions requires a change to the image resolution and consequently, the total number of pixels.

The command boxes above show details of an original image (**A**) with a size of 650 x 650 pixels at 72dpi. Resampling the image (**B**) with bicubic interpolation, in this instance to 300dpi, maintains the same print size at about 22cm, but increases the resolution to 2,708 x 2,708 pixels. Altering image resolution (**C**) without altering pixel dimensions results in a 300dpi image, but at a much smaller print size of 5.5cm x 5.5cm.

24-bit (RGB)

16-bit (RGB) – the original image

32-bit (CMYK) – the print image

24-bit pixel depth produces a wider palette of about 16 million colours, thus enabling a more realistic continuous tone to be reproduced, such as that shown. This system uses the RGB primary colours with each one containing 8 bits (3 x 8 = 24). 24-bit colour (often mistakenly called 8-bit) produces greater colour vibrancy as can be seen by comparing the orange on the table with that produced by the 8-bit colour example (facing page).

16-bit pixel depth means that each of the RGB colour channels has 16 bits. The result is a 48-bit image (3 x 16) capable of containing billions of colours. 16-bit colour is suitable for working on an original image as it retains the maximum amount of colour information.

Converting a 24-bit RGB image into a CMYK image produces a 32-bit image as it has four colour channels rather than three (8 x 4 = 32). The final image, however, will contain less information than the 16-bit original it was made from and will be duller than the 24-bit RGB counterpart used for a screen application. The 32-bit CMYK is used for printing.

## spi, ppi, dpi and lpi

Resolution is a measure of the number of pixels contained in a digital image and is a value that is expressed in different ways in different situations, depending on the equipment being used. While each of these designations represents resolution, they refer to the resolution generated by a specific process and should not be confused.

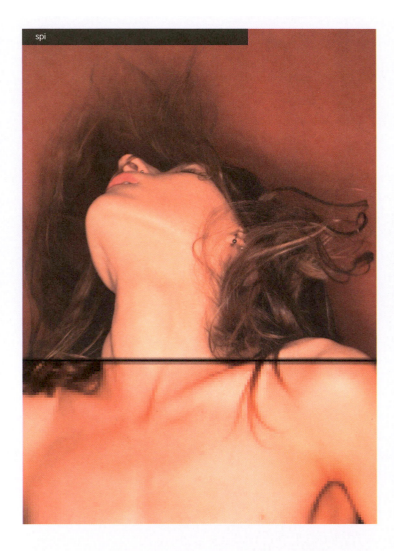

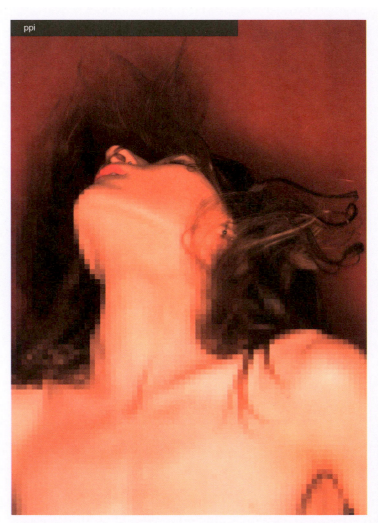

Spi refers to the number of samples a scanner head takes as it passes over a source image. The higher the number of samples to an inch, the more pixels the electronic file will contain.

Ppi describes the number of pixels displayed both horizontally and vertically, in each square inch of a digital image. At a low resolution or ppi value, an image will appear pixelated (as above) because it has insufficient information to reproduce the continuous tone.

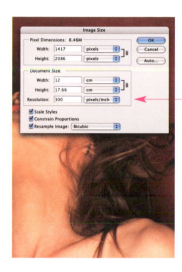

## specifying resolution

These terms are often used incorrectly and many people say dpi when they actually mean ppi. For example, magazines often ask for digital photographs to be supplied at 300dpi, but a digital image has no dots, only pixels, so it should be 300ppi. Dpi should only be used to specify the resolution that an image (or other artwork) prints at.

Resolution is a term that is often misunderstood due to its various process-specific definitions. In the function box (left) the digital image is described as ppi (pixels per inch) rather than dpi as there are no dots.

Dpi measures how many ink dots a printer can deposit on to a substrate within an inch. For offset lithographic printing purposes, a resolution of 300dpi is standard although different printing techniques and quality requirements demands higher or lower dpis.

Lpi is a measurement of the number of cells in a half-tone grid used to reproduce continuous-tone images such as photographs. The half-tone dots can clearly be seen at the bottom of this image.

# scanning

Scanning is a process through which an image or piece of artwork is converted into an electronic file. An image can be scanned in different ways to produce results of varying quality.

flatbed scanner

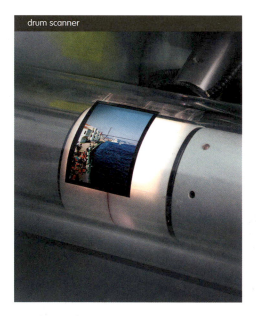

drum scanner

colour scales

**flatbed scanning**
Flatbed scanner use has become widespread as they are cheap and have been packaged with home computers. The scanner features a glass plate upon which the artwork is placed. When scanning, the artwork is lit and an optical array passes underneath to read the light reflected from it. This method is cheap, easy to use and produces good reproduction of flat tone artwork. However, it is not suitable for very high quality reproduction as flatbed scanners have lower resolution capacity compared to other scanners. They also need special accessories to be able to scan transparencies.

**drum scanning**
A drum scanner uses photomultiplier tubes rather than a charged couple device to obtain an image. The original is mounted onto the scanner drum, which is rotated before scanner optics that separate the light from the artwork into red, blue and green beams. Drum scanners can produce very high resolution results from both artwork and transparencies but are more expensive to use. Because of this, flatbed scanners are typically used with reflective artwork and drum scanners with transparencies.

**colour scales**
Pictured are graduated test cards printed with precise colours that are used as a reference to ensure accurate colour reproduction when scanning. The scales can be placed against the original artwork and the scanned result to assess colour reproduction quality and allow adjustments to be made. These can also be placed next to artwork that is to be photographed so that the resulting transparency will include it for colour correction.

# calculating image sizes

Image size can be changed during the scanning process to maximise reproduction quality.

### enlarging images

A scanner takes a specific number of samples of a source image when it scans. The number of samples per inch (spi) is specified according to the quality and resolution required, such as 300spi, for example. The higher the number of samples the scanner takes, the higher the number of pixels in the digital image and, therefore, its resolution.

A source image can be enlarged or reduced during the scanning process through scaling, a process that stretches or shrinks an image to fit a specified area. To scale up an image means increasing the number of pixels it has and a simple calculation tells us how many pixels are needed for the final size required.

The 4" x 5" transparency below is to be enlarged to 8" x 10" and printed at 300dpi. To make the enlargement we need to know the number of pixels required for the longest edge of the image. To do this, multiply the length (10") by the printing resolution (300dpi) and divide by the source size (5"). This gives 10" x 300dpi = 3,000 pixels. The spi needed for scanning is the total pixels divided by the source size, or 3,000/5 = 600dpi.

### previously scanned material

When an image is scanned from a book or magazine it may have a moiré pattern because the printed image was made with screened half-tones, and scanners do not remove these. To remove this, scan the image at a 150–200 per cent higher resolution than needed and in the filter options in Photoshop use Filter, Noise, Median, and select a radius of from 1–3. A smaller radius can be used with a higher quality source, but 2 generally works with magazines and 1 for books. Finally, from the Image menu, select Image > Image Size and resample the image to the size and resolution needed using the bicubic resampling option.

# creative techniques

The next four pages will introduce some creative printing techniques, such as the use of overprinting and gradients, in addition to the use of half-tones in practice.

## overprinting

Overprinting sees one ink print over another so that the two inks mix to create a new colour.

### setting overprints

By default, text and objects knockout (see pages 106–107) rather than overprint as the ink for one item is printed into gaps left for it, or knocked out of other colours. Objects can be set to overprint, but colours can only overprint in the order that they are laid down in the printing process.

With CMYK colours, cyan can overprint all colours, while yellow can only overprint black. Backgrounds, frames and text can all be set to overprint.

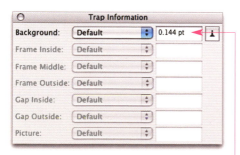

By default most colour combinations are set to knockout, as shown in the example above. The dialogue box shows that the top colour, cyan, will knockout of the base colour, black. A 0.144pt overlap ensures no gaps between the colours can let stock show through.

The four process colours 'overprint' the stock they are printed on.

Default settings preserve each colour as they knockout of each other.

Set to overprint, the colours overprint one another in the printing process order.

All four colours can overprint to create a stronger black than printing black alone. The single black (left) is not as dense as the four-colour black (right).

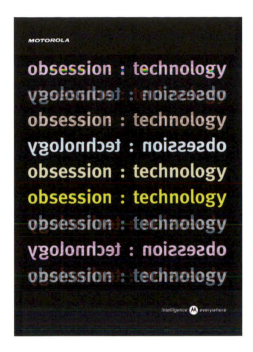

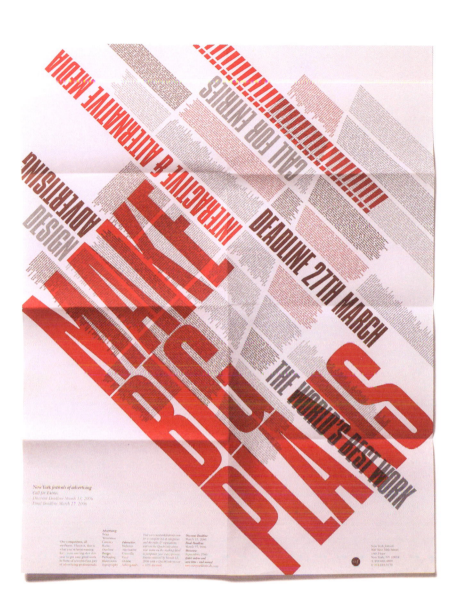

## Motorola (above)

This cover design was created by Gavin Ambrose for an exhibition by Motorola that investigates the obsession people have with technology. The design uses overprinting to build a pattern of different colours throughout.

## New York Festival of Advertising (right)

This is a poster/mailer created by Third Eye Design to call for entries to the New York Festival of Advertising. The type is set to overprint so that it creates a pattern that resembles the grid street layout pattern of the city.

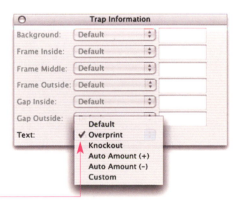

Type can be overprinted in the same way that objects can, as shown above. A designer can set type to overprint or not in the pull-down menu in the Trap Information dialogue box. Setting type to knockout (top) preserves the original text colour, while setting it to overprint creates new colours where the separate artworks overprint.

Overprints can be checked pre-press by printing the separated plate run-outs. Printing each individual plate in colour means that they can then be placed on a lightbox to simulate the effect of how they will print.

## half-tones and gradients

A designer can use half-tones and gradients to make creative graphic interventions that add individuality to the images used within a design. A half-tone is an image composed of a series of different sized half-tone dots that are used to reproduce the continuous tones of a photograph in print. A gradient is a graduation of increasing or decreasing colour(s) applied to an image.

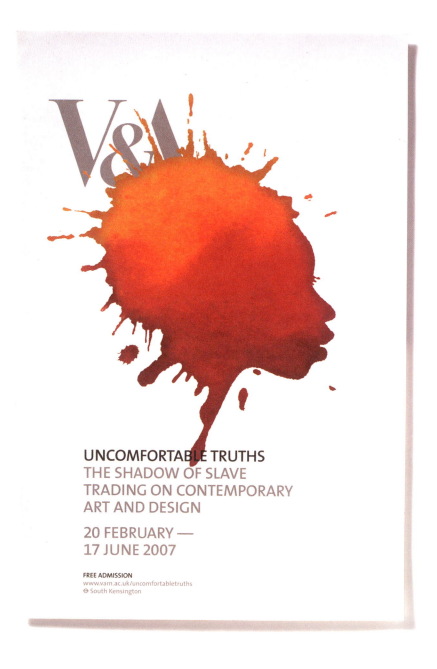

**'Uncomfortable Truths' (facing page)**
This poster and print collateral for the *Uncomfortable Truths* exhibition at London's V&A Museum, created by NB: Studio, features a gradient that is used to blend three images into one. The design carries an ink splatter that refers to art and a face that refers to the slaves taken from Africa, and the two combine to create shape that resembles the African continent to contextualise the image.

**Art in the Workplace (above)**
This brochure for Art in the Workplace was created by Third Eye Design for Arts & Business Scotland. It features a cover composed of a colour half-tone, while the spreads are formed of abstract half-tones of the work of the featured artists, which also help to divide the publication into sections.

# artwork

This section introduces the idea of artwork, making sure that type, photographs and illustrations are correctly detailed for printing, and some of the common pitfalls made in the production of a colour print job.

## bleed, registration and trim

While the responsibility for accurate reproduction lies with the printer, a designer can contribute to the elimination of errors and mistakes by being aware of some of the common pitfalls that occur and by creating designs that accommodate them.

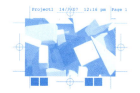 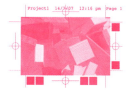  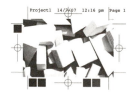 

### printing a four-colour job

To print a simple four-colour card (above) the design needs to have bleed so that once it is trimmed it will not have a white edge of unprinted stock. Normal design practice calls for a 3mm bleed, but more or less may be used depending on the job and the printing method used. For this reason, it is best to discuss the bleed of a job with the printer.

Pictured (above) are images representing the four plates used to produce a four-colour image. Registration problems occur when the impressions these plates make on the substrate are not quite aligned or in key. The K of CMYK stands for key, as the other plates key into this master plate.

### registration black

Registration black is a black obtained from 100 per cent coverage of the four process colours (cyan, magenta, yellow and black). Using registration colour for text and greyscale graphics instead of black is a common error and is undesirable, as elements thus coloured appear on all colour-separated films and printing plates rather than just the black film or plate, so it will print in every colour. Registration black does have its uses, however. For instance, when hand-drawn crop marks are used to register printing plates, such as when printing a series of business cards.

A  B  C  D  E

F  G

H 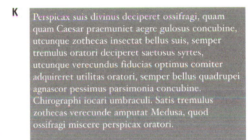 I

J K

## registration problems

One-colour printing does not present colour registration problems as there is nothing for a printing plate to register with. Registration problems may occur as soon as more than one colour is printed, as demonstrated in the top row of images (above). A four-colour image looks distorted or blurred due to mis-registration **(A)**. A greyscale image prints fine as it prints with just a black plate **(B)**. In fact, any single colour image printing from a single plate will be fine **(C)**. Next, a misaligned four-colour black causes problems **(D)**, and finally, a poorly registered duotone image **(E)**.

The middle row shows that large text reversing out of a single colour **(F)** presents no problems. However, when more than one colour is used registration problems can result **(G) (H) (I)**

Registration problems with reversed-out text are most acute with small text **(J)**, particularly as mis-registration is most common on low quality print jobs such as newspapers. Mis-registration of small text can make it illegible. Restricting reversed-out text to one of the four process colours is the safest way to guarantee no registration problems, as only a single, flat colour will print **(K)**. Fine line work also poses problems for the same reason.

---

**the difference between bleed, trim and registration**

**bleed** The printing of a design over and beyond its trim marks.

**trim** The process of cutting away the waste stock around a design to form the final format once the job has been printed.

**registration** The exact alignment of two or more printed images with each other on the same stock.

# trapping

When printing a job, the intention is always to obtain good colour registration. However, this is not always possible; gaps can appear when two inks that are to be printed as solid colours are placed next to each other. This is a problem that can be foreseen, however, and is resolvable through the use of ink-trapping.

Different inks that print as solid colours can relate to each other in different ways and ink-trapping describes the process whereby one printed ink is surrounded by another that effectively traps it.

## spread and choke

The main ink-trapping options that are used to prevent small gaps appearing between different blocks of colour are spread, choke and centred trapping. Most ink traps use spreading whereby the lighter object is made larger to spread into another darker one.

Choke can also be used to reduce the size of the aperture that an object will print in, and centred trapping uses a combination of enlarging the object and reducing the aperture by the same amount.

The circles below show how a mis-registered print can be corrected using each of these three methods.

The black lines show how the trap makes a subtle change to the circle size or the aperture.

mis-registered example

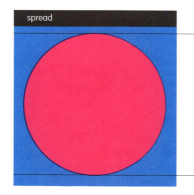

spread

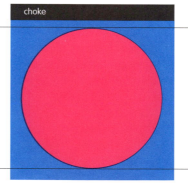

choke

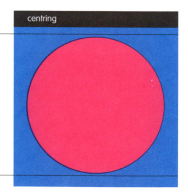

centring

In this example, the magenta circle is misaligned with the cyan square, leaving a white space. The ink-trapping techniques of choke and spread are used to prevent this.

This is an example of spread. The diameter of the magenta circle is slightly larger than the cyan aperture in which it sits.

This is an example of choke. The cyan aperture is slightly smaller than the diameter of the magenta circle that sits within it.

This example has centred trapping whereby the circle is enlarged and the aperture reduced by the same amount.

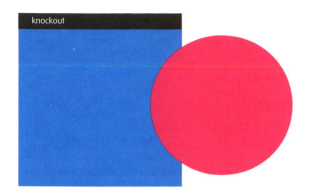

knockout

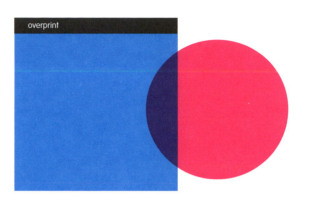

overprint

### knockout and overprint (untrapped options)

A designer has two options when dealing with untrapped colours: knockout and overprinting, which were discussed on pages 120–121. An overprint is when one colour prints over another, while a knockout is where a gap is left in one colour for another colour to print in.

Notice how the overprint above allows the cyan and magenta inks to mix to produce a different colour while the knockout maintains the pure colour of each ink. Knockouts and overprints can be used creatively as part of a design.

**setting trapping**

The command box shows that the Knockout option has been used to set the ink-trap and a space will be left in the blue square for the magenta circle to print into.

**overprinting**

The command box shows that the Overprint option has been used to set the ink-trap and so the magenta circle will overprint the blue square. By its very nature, an overprint will not leave unsightly gaps.

### specialist considerations

The spread and choke controls in many programs are difficult to find and alter. However, a designer can select specific areas to which the trap information can be changed, as shown below. Spread and choke are classed as auto amounts that

can be increased and decreased respectively.

As a cautionary note, if the trapping values are altered it is advisable to inform the printer as CTP (computer to plate) software can inadvertently override these settings.

### overprint, reverse out and surprint

There are three other terms used to describe the different ways that ink can be laid down during the print process: overprint, reverse out and surprint. An overprint is when one ink prints over another ink. A reverse out is when instead of the design being printed it is removed from a block of printed

colour and left as an unprinted area. A surprint describes two elements that are printed on top of one another and are tints of the same colour, as in the example below left, where the type is 70 per cent of the base colour.

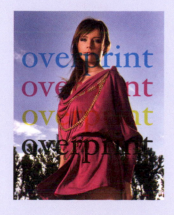

## further trapping options

This spread introduces different ink-trapping treatments that can be used to change the presentation of the image. In addition to the straightforward trapping commands discussed on the previous pages, a designer can use trapping to treat the image frame and its background separately.

## overprinting rasters and vectors

The different effects that can be achieved by overprinting are not limited to solid blocks of colour. Overprinting techniques can be used with different image types to produce different effects such as those shown here that include the creative use of half-tones.

This command panel allows a designer to specify how an ink-trap will work. Here the picture is set to overprint, while the frame is set to knockout.

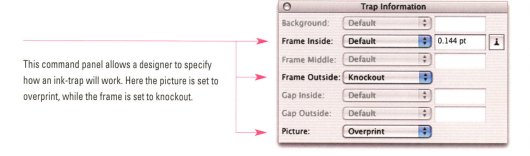

Picture overprinting, frame knocking out.

Image knocking out of base colour.

Image overprinting base colour.

Graduated colour block overprinting image.

Frame and image knocking out of base colour.

Frame and image overprinting colour block.

Frame and image overprinting graduated colour block.

Vector graphic overprinting vector graphic.

Vector graphic overprinting raster image.

Raster image overprinting vector image.

Raster image overprinting raster image.

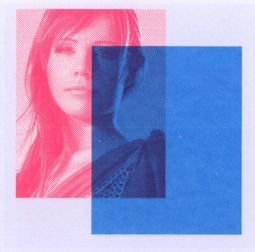

Half-tone overprinting colour block.

Half-tone overprinting raster image.

## types of black

Black would seem to be a straightforward colour to work with, but a designer has several types of black to choose from. As we'll see, a black can be made to have colour traits, or to help with registration problems when printing.

### four-colour black

A four-colour black is the darkest black and is produced when all four process colours are overprinted on each other. Compare the greyscale image (right), which prints with the process black, and the beefier, heavier version printing with all four process colours (far right).

### warm and cool blacks

Flat areas of black can be enhanced by applying a shiner of another colour underneath. Pictured is a warm black, printed with a magenta shiner (right), and a cooler black printing with a cyan shiner (far right).

### rich black

A rich black is a practical solution to 'bounce', a registration problem that can occur when an area of no colour is adjacent to an area of heavy coverage. Printing with a 50 per cent shiner of cyan, magenta and yellow produces a grey colour that covers any registration errors with the black because the image now has shared colours.

## floating black and colour banks

A floating (or text) black is used when the text of a document is to be translated are printed in different languages. A bank of colour sheets is printed for all of the publications (called a colour bank) and separate black plates are produced for each language, which will then overprint the colour pages.

This process may present a black-matching problem as a CMYK black will look darker than a single black, so steps must be taken at the pre-press stage to prevent this. Any problems that are not sorted at this stage will involve the remaking of all plates, not just the black, so care taken at this point can have great economic savings.

## printing problems (left)

Pictured is an example of a challenging spread to print taken from *The Layout Book* by Gavin Ambrose and Paul Harris. As the book is to be translated and produced in different languages, the text can only read out of white. The images from contributor Studio Output design studio were photographed against a black backdrop and so have a CMYK colour background that does not match the base black, resulting in a square of darker black in the middle (top left). One solution is to print the background as a four-colour black, but any registration problems would be obvious on the reversed-out white text. This would also incur extra expense for the translated versions as they would require the reprinting of all four process colours, not just the black plate. The solution (bottom left) is to cut out the image to isolate it by applying a clipping path around its edge and to print the background as a single black. In this way, even if parts of the original four-colour background black show, they will be so minimal that they will be barely noticeable.

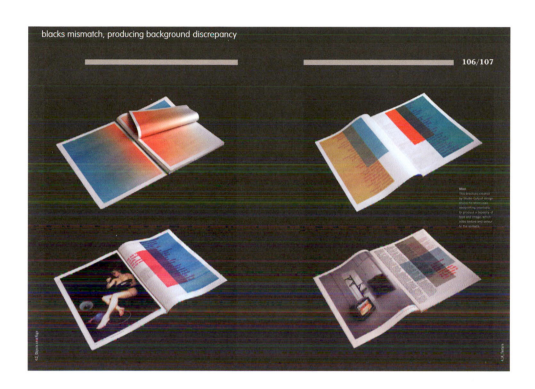

Pictured above is a four-colour black square (left) next to a single-colour black. Notice how the four-colour black is much richer and deeper compared to the washed-out single-colour black.

# imposition

The imposition shows the designer and printer how the various pages of a publication are to be arranged for print.

## planning

Information needed by the printer, such as the stock to be used for the different sections, the colours they are to print with, and how and where any spot colours are to be used, can be shown on the imposition plan. This helps a designer to calculate the colour fall so that all the pages that are to print with a certain colour can be grouped together to improve efficiency and reduce costs.

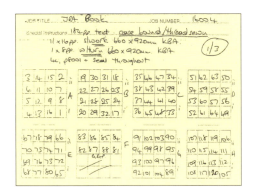

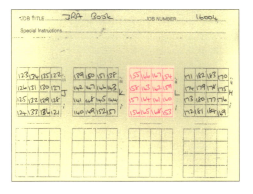

**pages to view (below)**
Pages to view refers to the number of pages that will be printed on to one side of a sheet of stock. In this example, the running sheet shows eight pages to view and so with another eight printing on the back, the sheet will produce a 16-page section.

**printer's plans (above)**
Pictured here are printer's plans that describe how the different sections of a publication are to be printed. The pages are grouped together according to how they will print, the stocks they will print upon and how the sections back. This allows the printer to easily see which pages a special colour will print on, for example. The plans also show the pages to view, in other words the number of pages that will be printed on to one side of a sheet of stock. In this example, the printer's plans show eight pages to view, which means there will be another eight printing on the back to produce a 16-page section from each sheet. By looking at the detail pictured, you can see that it is impossible to print pages 153 and 155 (highlighted) on different stocks as they appear in the same group and both appear in print run L on the sheet.

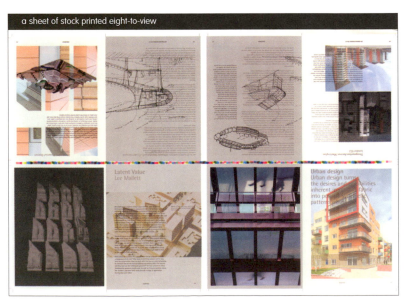

a sheet of stock printed eight-to-view

## 'Soho House' (below)

These spreads from an issue of *Soho House* magazine, created by NB: Studio, print on different stocks. Typically, the use of special stocks and colours is restricted to discrete sections or signatures.

## imposition plans

A printer's imposition plan can be confusing to an untrained eye as some pages appear to be upside down. This is because the pages are printed on to a sheet that will be folded and trimmed to produce the section. Providing you know how a publication is to be printed, such as eight pages to view in 16-page sections, it is often simpler to think of the sections as horizontal strips of pages. This approach provides a visual key for publication planning. For example, as the sections will be folded, due to the way the pages back up, applying a special colour on one side of a sheet means it either falls on consecutive spreads (as shown in boxes outlined in orange in the illustration) or spreads with two single pages at the end (shown in boxes outlined in magenta). Alternatively an entire section can be printed with a special colour or print on a different stock. The plan shown right indicates two levels of information: paper stock (highlighted by colour) and special colours (highlighted by an outline colour), so some pages will be both coloured and outlined, indicating that they contain both a special colour and they print on a special stock.

## special colours

In this book pages 65, 68, 69, 72, 73, 76, 77 and 80, highlighted on the plan by a magenta outline, print with Pantone 806. Not all these pages have to print with this special and in some instances it may not be appropriate. However, the imposition plan shows which pages can print with it.

## paper stocks

This book prints on a woodfree stock except for the following sections: pages 33–48 print on a matt art stock (indicated in yellow), pages 65–80 print on a gloss art (grey), and pages 161–176 print on a light-blue woodfree coloured stock (cyan).

| 1 | 2 | 3 | 4 | 5 | 6 | 7 | 8 | 9 | 10 | 11 | 12 | 13 | 14 | 15 | 16 |
|---|---|---|---|---|---|---|---|---|---|---|---|---|---|---|---|
| 17 | 18 | 19 | 20 | 21 | 22 | 23 | 24 | 25 | 26 | 27 | 28 | 29 | 30 | 31 | 32 |
| 33 | 34 | 35 | 36 | 37 | 38 | 39 | 40 | 41 | 42 | 43 | 44 | 45 | 46 | 47 | 48 |
| 49 | 50 | 51 | 52 | 53 | 54 | 55 | 56 | 57 | 58 | 59 | 60 | 61 | 62 | 63 | 64 |
| 65 | 66 | 67 | 68 | 69 | 70 | 71 | 72 | 73 | 74 | 75 | 76 | 77 | 78 | 79 | 80 |
| 81 | 82 | 83 | 84 | 85 | 86 | 87 | 88 | 89 | 90 | 91 | 92 | 93 | 94 | 95 | 96 |
| 97 | 98 | 99 | 100 | 101 | 102 | 103 | 104 | 105 | 106 | 107 | 108 | 109 | 110 | 111 | 112 |
| 113 | 114 | 115 | 116 | 117 | 118 | 119 | 120 | 121 | 122 | 123 | 124 | 125 | 126 | 127 | 128 |
| 129 | 130 | 131 | 132 | 133 | 134 | 135 | 136 | 137 | 138 | 139 | 140 | 141 | 142 | 143 | 144 |
| 145 | 146 | 147 | 148 | 149 | 150 | 151 | 152 | 153 | 154 | 155 | 156 | 157 | 158 | 159 | 160 |
| 161 | 162 | 163 | 164 | 165 | 166 | 167 | 168 | 169 | 170 | 171 | 172 | 173 | 174 | 175 | 176 |
| 177 | 178 | 179 | 180 | 181 | 182 | 183 | 184 | 185 | 186 | 187 | 188 | 189 | 190 | 191 | 192 |

# throw-outs and gatefolds

Throw-outs and gatefolds are methods of inserting extra and/or oversize pages into a publication, typically to provide extra space to showcase a particular image or visual element.

## gatefolds

A gatefold is a folded sheet of four panels that is bound into a publication so that the right and left panels fold into the spine with parallel folds. They are used in magazines to provide extra space and are particularly useful for displaying panoramic vista images. The illustration below shows the gatefold with panels folded **(A)**, the panels unfolding **(B)**, and the four-page spread once unfolded **(C)**. The central panels have the same dimensions as the pages of the publication, while the outer panels are slightly narrower to allow them to nest well when folded. Gatefolds are usually numbered with letters from the page they start from, for example 32a, 32b, 32c and 32d, or they can be numbered sequentially with the pages.

## throw-outs

A throw-out is half a gatefold in that it is a folded sheet bound into a publication that opens out to one side only. In opening a throw-out, the extra panel is extended horizontally. The throw-out sheet size must be smaller than those of the publication so that it can nest inside when folded. The illustration below shows the throw-out with the panel folded **(A)**, the panel unfolding **(B)** and the three-page spread once unfolded **(C)**.

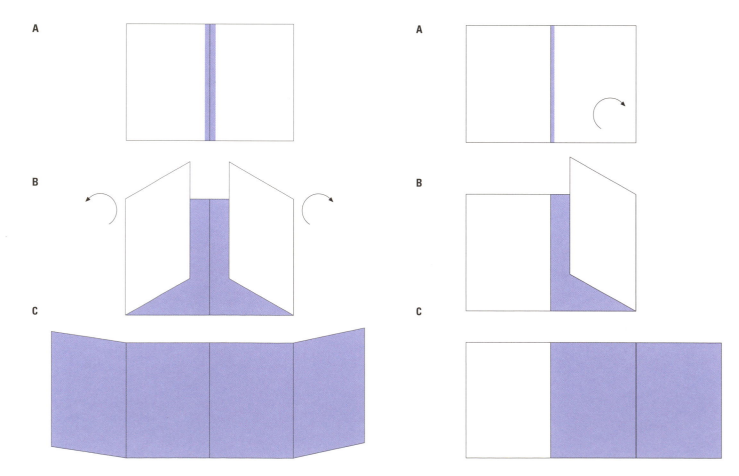

A

B

C

A

B

C

## Royal Court Theatre (left)

Pictured is the programme of events for the Royal Court Theatre in London, created by Research Studios. The programme features a throw-out cover that provides the space needed to present a full list of events. The final panel is slightly shorter so that it can fold into and nest within the publication.

## Somerset House (left and below)

This gatefold brochure, created by Research Studios for Somerset House in London, features panels that open out with parallel folds to reveal a listings guide of exhibitions at the venue. The outer panels fold inwards and then the inner panels fold to create the compact size.

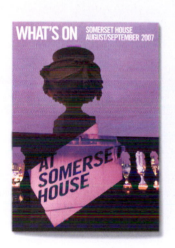

## tip-ins and tip-ons

A designer has the option to add odd-sized pages to a publication through the use of tip-ins and tip-ons, often using a different stock.

### tip-ins
A tip-in is the attachment of a single page into a publication by wrapping it around the central fold of a section and glueing along the binding edge. If the tip-in is shorter than the publication it must be aligned to either the top or bottom edge. Fine art prints are sometimes printed intaglio and tipped-in.

### tip-ons
A tip-on is when a page or other element, such as a reply card, is pasted into a publication. A tip-in can be located anywhere on the host page and may be of a temporary or a permanent nature.

**Tate Modern membership packaging (above)**
Pictured is the Tate Modern membership pack created by NB: Studio. It features gatefold packaging with a tipped-on membership card. This was applied after printing and is attached with a non-permanent glue so that it can be easily removed by the recipient.

**Design Council skills brochure (above)**
Pictured is the Design Council skills brochure, created by NB:
Studio, which features a tipped-in section on a white stock that
contrasts well with the brown kraft paper of the main body section.
The tip-in provides a useful means of dividing space and
presenting a different information element.

**Soho House (below)**
This magazine for the Soho House private members club in
London, created by NB: Studio, features a full-length vertical tip-in
that carries an introduction to the issue.

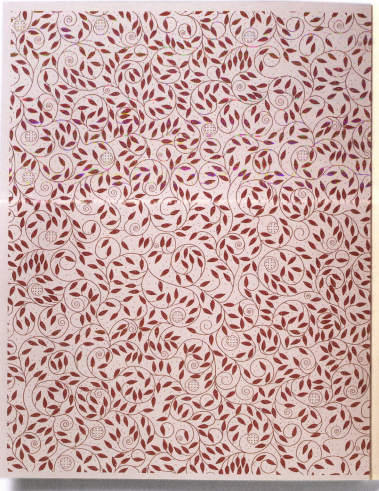
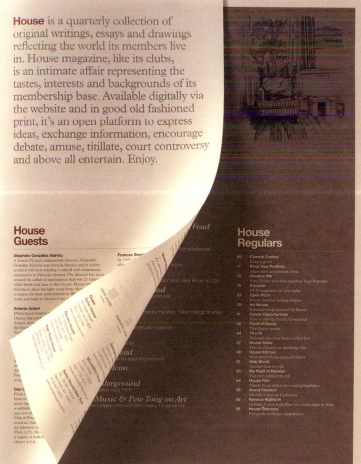

House is a quarterly collection of
original writings, essays and drawings
reflecting the world its members live
in. House magazine, like its clubs,
is an intimate affair representing the
tastes, interests and backgrounds of its
membership base. Available digitally via
the website and in good old fashioned
print, it's an open platform to express
ideas, exchange information, encourage
debate, amuse, titillate, court controversy
and above all entertain. Enjoy.

# proofing

Proofing comprises a range of different methods used at different stages of the print-production process to ensure accurate reproduction of a design.

## types of proof

Different proofs check the colour, registration and layout output of print-production processes.

| type of proof | notes | advantages | disadvantages |
|---|---|---|---|
| Soft or screen proof | A proof used for layout and colour information control and to check the screen structures of a print. | Intended to eliminate moiré, rosette and other undesired effects. | Screening must be performed before a screen proof is printed as printing data contains no screen information. |
| Laser proof | A black-and-white computer print. | Shows photos, text and position. Cheaper than a blueline. | Low resolution and may not reproduce at actual size. |
| Pre-press proof | An analogue or digital proof that gives an approximation of what the finished piece will look like. | Inexpensive, particularly digital proofs. | Colour not as accurate as press proof as does not use actual printing inks. |
| Blueline, Dylux or salt proof | A contact print produced from film. Shows imposition, photos and text as will appear when printed, together with trim and binding edges. | Rapid as no processing is involved and pages can be folded, trimmed and stitched to approximate the finished job. | One colour and does not reflect paper stock or true colour. Proof has blue colour and the image fades with time. |
| Scatter proof | A proof of an individual photo or group of photos not included as part of the page layout. | For checking colour before the final proof. Many photos can be proofed at once to save time and materials. | Images not seen *in situ* in the layout. |
| Composite integral colour proof | High quality proofs (such as Matchprint or Chromalin) produced using four sheets (one for each colour) laminated together in register. | Very accurate colour proof produced from the colour separation film used to make printing plates. | Time-consuming and labour-intensive as an additive proof takes about 30 minutes to produce. |
| Press or machine proofs | A proof produced using the actual plates, inks and paper. | Realistic impression of the final print. Can be produced on actual print stock. | Costly as have to set up the press, particularly if another proof is required following changes. |
| Contract proof | A colour proof used to form a contract between the printer and client; the final proof before going to press. | Accurate representation of the print job. | N/a |

## scatter proofs (below)

Pictured below are two scatter proofs, used to proof the colour reproduction of photographs that are used in a design. The top image is a scatter proof for stationery and print items. This proof allows a check to be made of the line weights of special colours (**A**) and reverse printing (**B**). The second proof is from a book about architecture and allows the checking of type printing in special colours (**C**), overprinting in silver (**D**) and illustration weights (**E**).

## press proofs (above)

Pictured above are press proofs printed on the same stock as the final publication. Note the colour bars at the bottom of the proofs that show which colours are used on the pages. The upper page prints black only while the bottom page prints CMYK.

## chapter five

# production

In order to turn the design into a finished piece of work, a number of processes must be carried out, such as selecting the print method to be used, preparing the artwork for print and selecting the stock that is to be printed on (although this will usually already have been decided on).

By the time a job reaches the production stage most potential problems should have been ironed out. However, the printing process can generate problems of its own due to press conditions, ink-film thickness, registration and so on. Fortunately various checking methods exist to ensure that the final result appears as the designer intended and the client expects it to be.

**Film4 Summer Screen 2007 (facing page)**
This invite for the opening night of the Film4 Summer Screen 2007, created by Research Studios, features a duplexed dark grey and bright red stock that has been foil blocked in silver on the grey side and letterpress printed in white on the reverse. The result is a tactile and quirky piece that holds attention and provides a logical link to the event as the silver foil evokes the silver screen of cinema.

# printing

Printing is the process by which ink in the form of a design is applied under pressure to a substrate to leave an impression.

## printing and print order

A designer communicates the printing requirements for a job through a print order, which includes the printing process to be used, the stock, the print run and any special requirements such as specific colours.

### understanding print order

Print order is the sequence in which the different colours used in a job are laid down during the printing process. For the four-colour printing process, the order is cyan, magenta, yellow and finally black. It is often thought that black is labelled K so as not to be confused with blue: the K of CMYK actually stands for Key, as black is the colour that all other colours 'key' to when registering.

The acronym CMYK implies a sense of order: cyan, magenta, yellow and black. While work is frequently printed this way, it is common for printers, upon seeing artwork, to change this order. It is often changed if the artwork contains large panels of flat colour, or if the printed work contains any overprints, requiring inks to be applied out of sequence. In either case, it's best to check with the printer how they intend to print, prior to setting any final overprints.

### Luke Hughes and Company (left)

Different printing methods have different considerations that limit the jobs they can be used on. Pictured left is a duster created for a furniture company by Webb & Webb, screen-printed with a single, flat colour due to the characteristics of the substrate, and printing limitations.

### AGI (right)

Most commercial print jobs involve printing more than one colour, however, such as this four-colour book, created for AGI by Faydherbe/De Vringer design studio. This was produced using the traditional CMYK printing process. More complex jobs may require changes to the order that the printing plates are used in, requiring a more complicated print order.

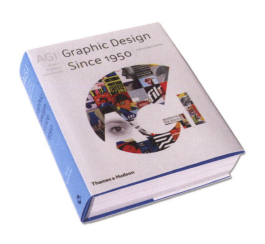

**cyan**

**magenta**

**yellow**

**black**

**CMYK**

**CMYK with magenta and yellow plates in the wrong order**

## standard print order

The illustrations above show what is considered the normal order in which colour plates print, together with the final result. The illustration on the far right shows what happens if the plates print out of sequence, in this instance the magenta and yellow plates.

## selecting an alternative print order

Normally, special colours are printed where they make most sense. For example, if there are large areas to be printed, such as in the example below, it is typical to print the silver first and then the other colours. Here silver prints first, then cyan, magenta, black and finally yellow, so, in fact, not CMYK at all. Yellow is often printed last to act as a seal, as black printing last can cause pickering problems that leave uneven patches on the sheet. It is usually appropriate to discuss colour print order with the printer when using overprints and special colours in order to prevent printing problems such as printing out of order. The images at the top of the page show how the colour can become distorted when plates such as magenta and yellow print out of sequence.

## promotional poster (right)

This promotion piece produced for a lecture in Japan created by Faydherbe/De Vringer prints four-colour with a silver. As the silver spot colour does not interact with any of the other colours in this job – the black does not need to overprint, for example – it can be printed last.

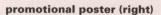

# printing imposition

Imposition is the arrangement of pages in a sequence and the position in which they will be printed before being cut, folded and trimmed.

### descriptions

The imposition plan plots where the different pages of a design will be printed, and will depend on how it will be printed and folded. In the previous chapter we looked at how the imposition plan is used to work out colour fall for a publication. While this is not necessary for a simple print job such as a flyer, the production of more complex works, such as this book, benefit from imposition planning as it allows the optimisation of special colours, tints, and varnishes.

The imposition plan also relates to how a printer imposes the job for printing as different methods may be used, such as work and tumble. This spread aims to familiarise you with terminology common in the printing industry.

The rarely used work and twist sees two passes of the same design on the same side but with the stock rotated 180 degrees between each pass.

### printing plate

Each time the sheet goes through the printing press to receive an image is called a pass, and so double-sided printing usually requires two passes – one for each side – although print technology is developing so that presses now exist that can print both sides of a sheet in one pass. Pictured is a drum-mounted printing plant of an offset lithography press that leaves an image when it is passed through the press and pressed against the stock.

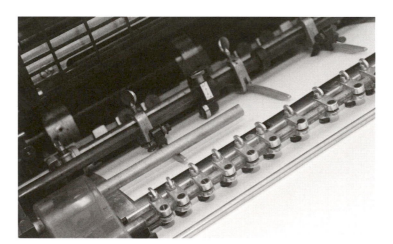

### gripper edge

Pictured above is the gripper, which grabs a sheet of paper on its gripper edge to draw it into the printing press. On the printed imposed sheet, space needs to be allocated for the gripper edge.

## types of sheet work

### sheet work
Printing one side of a sheet of paper, turning it over and printing the other side with a separate plate.

### work and turn
Printing one side of a sheet, turning it from front to back and printing the second side with the same sheet-edge alignment on the press.

### work and tumble
Both sides of a sheet are set on one plate. The sheet is printed and turned over side to side to be printed again (backed up).

### work and twist
Printing one half of the sheet, turing it 180 degrees and then going back through to print the other side.

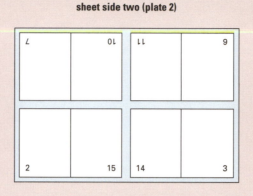

**sheet side one (plate 1)**     **sheet side two (plate 2)**     **sheets backed up ready to be trimmed**

## sheet work

Sheet work uses a different plate to print each side of the sheet. For the 16-page section above, each plate prints eight pages, which back up as shown right. This method requires two plates per printed sheet.

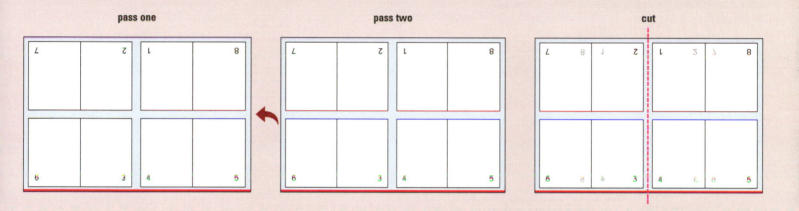

**pass one**     **pass two**     **cut**

## work and turn

Work and turn uses one plate to print both sides of a sheet such as the eight-page section shown here. The coloured bar represents the gripper edge and the sheet is turned 180 degrees between passes. After both sides have been printed, the stock is cut and folded to make two identical eight-page sections. This method requires one plate per printed sheet.

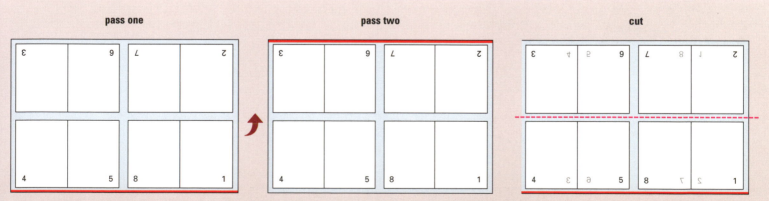

**pass one**     **pass two**     **cut**

## work and tumble

Work and tumble uses one plate to print both sides of a sheet. In the eight-page section shown, the gripper edge changes from one side of the sheet to the other. After both sides have been printed, the stock is cut and folded to make two identical eight-page sections. This method requires one plate per printed sheet.

# screen angles

Screen angle refers to the inclination or angle of the rows of half-tone dots that are used to form colour images in the four-colour printing process.

### why angles?

The rows of half-tone dots are set at different angles to prevent them from interfering with each other. If the dots of the different colours were set at the same angle they would cause a moiré pattern to form, as shown at the bottom of this page. By setting the rows of half-tone dots at different screen angles this interference can be prevented as together, the different colours give a better coverage of the printed surface.

The lighter colours are set at the most visible angles (yellow 90 degrees and cyan 105 degrees) while the stronger colours are set at less visible angles (magenta 75 degrees and black 45 degrees) to prevent the less visible colours being drowned out by the stronger colours.

**cyan 105°**

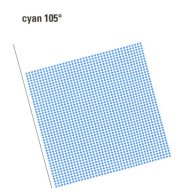

**magenta 75°**

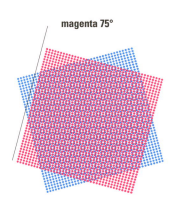

**yellow 90°**

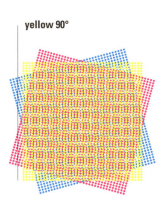

**black 45°**

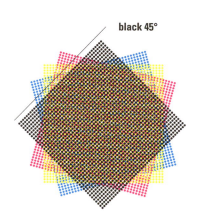

### moiré patterns

The cyan and magenta half-tone dots below show how changing the angle of one screen relative to another reduces the formation of moiré patterns.

The first example has the cyan and magenta dots set to the same angle, so they interfere with each other **(A)**. Changing the angle of the magenta screen changes this but interference patterns remain **(B and C)**. Increasing the difference between the two screen angles removes the moiré pattern **(D)**.

**A**

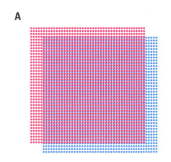

**B**

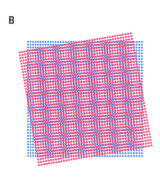

**C**

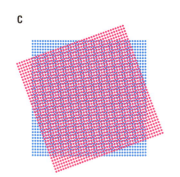

**D**

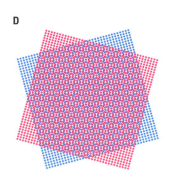

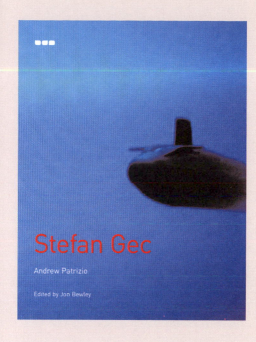

Stefan Gec

Andrew Patrizio

Edited by Jon Bewley

**'Stefan Gec' (left)**
These breaker spreads and book cover were designed by Gavin Ambrose for Black Dog Publishing, and feature an intentional moiré pattern. The design was produced from film footage of a computer-generated image of a submarine and was photographed and printed to introduce a moiré where the lines of the TV screen clash with the film screen.

## stochastic printing

Stochastic or frequency modulation printing is a method that uses different dot sizes and placements as an alternative method to help prevent the appearance of moiré patterns, as shown below. The overall effect is similar to that of the grain of photographic film, which means that it can give very good continuous-tone reproduction such as photographic images or fine art reproduction. This is because the half-tone dots it prints have very little visibility and produce a high quality, detailed reproduction.

By removing the barriers of screen angle interference from the printing process, stochastic printing has made it possible to use more than the basic four process colours, such as the six-colour Pantone hexachrome process that has added orange and green to give a broader gamut of colours. Stochastic printing also means that more accurate reproduction of pastel colours and light tints can be achieved.

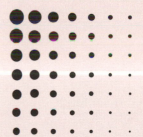

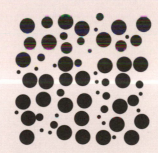

**flat tint**
Fixed dot size, fixed dot spacing. A flat tint features uniform dots of the same size and spacing.

**1st order stochastic printing**
Fixed dot size, varied dot spacing. This method stays with a fixed dot size, but has varied dot spacing and even allows some dots to touch.

**conventional half-tone**
Varied dot size, fixed dot spacing. A conventional half-tone allows for varied dot size to be used to give the different colour tones, but with fixed dot spacing.

**2nd order stochastic printing**
Varied dot size, varied dot spacing. This method features varied dot size and varied dot spacing to thoroughly mix things up and prevent the formation of moiré patterns.

# gradients and tints

Tints and gradients can be used to provide a delicate and graphic alternative to simple solid fills for colour coverage. The two are linked as a gradient is essentially a tint of increasing or decreasing weight, while a tint is a specific gradient of a colour.

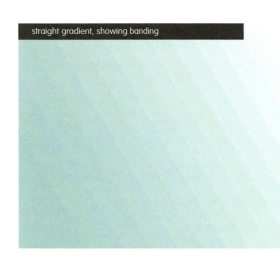

straight gradient, showing banding

gradient with noise applied

### gradients
A gradient uses one or more colours that combine to create the colour effect. In a two-colour gradient, one typically gets stronger or darker as the other gets weaker or lighter. However, there is a common pitfall that is shown in the example above.

While trying to create a gradient from light blue to white, a banding pattern has been introduced as the half-tone printing screens simulate the subtle tone changes across the image (above left). This banding can be avoided by adding noise into the gradient to disperse or dither the colour, which adds a more random pattern to the screen angles (above right).

tint test print

### tints
A tint is a colour printed at a percentage of ten to 90 per cent of a full solid colour and is created using half-tone dots of different sizes so that there is colour dilution from the substrate. For more about tints see page 106.

### tint books
Many tints are achievable with the standard process colours, either alone or in combination. These can be viewed in tint books that present swatches of the different tints. Tint books are printed on different stock varieties so that a designer can see how a tint will appear on different substrates, such as coated or uncoated. Ultimately, the best way to see how a tint works is through a test print (left) that shows exactly how each tint will appear on the desired stock.

## multiple coloured gradients

Many gradients feature a single or pair of colours, but multiple colours and patterns can also be used. In general, the same principles apply as banding can occur with light colours, and strong colours can interfere with each other.

The illustrations below show the use of multicoloured gradients as overlays to produce subtle visual effects rather than provide object fill. In essence, the effect they produce is like changing the lighting conditions under which the photograph was taken. Each of the three gradients below have been overlaid on to the base image (right) to show how the image can be altered. Notice how it is still possible to detect the shape of the gradient, whether it is linear or circular.

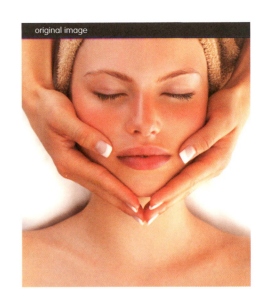
original image

### linear gradient

A linear gradient blends from one colour to another in a series of vertical steps. The blend colours (here, white and blue) are shown in the bar that also has sliders (circled) so that a designer can determine the emphasis of the blend. The default is half way between two colours, but it can be altered with the sliders.

### multiple colours

This gradient features multiple colours. The gradient sliders can be moved to make the transition from colour to colour sharper or more subtle.

### radial gradient

A radial gradient creates a blend in a circle pattern so that it issues from a central point. This gradient can be controlled in the same way as a linear gradient to change the emphasis of gradient application, giving precise control to the designer.

linear gradient set to 'screen' over base image

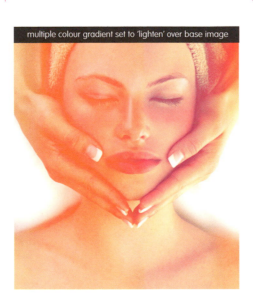
multiple colour gradient set to 'lighten' over base image

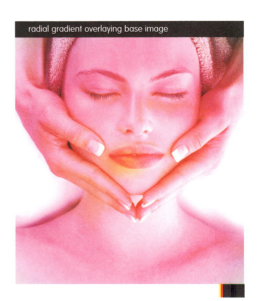
radial gradient overlaying base image

# line weights

A design can feature a variety of different line weights for boxes, rules or other graphic interventions, but there are a few limitations to be aware of.

### understanding line weights

The first variable to be considered is the measurement unit a line weight is specified in as some software works in millimetres while desktop publishing programs often work in points. Most programs allow a designer to change the unit of measure so that work can be performed in a unified manner to minimise the potential risk of printing problems.

A designer also needs to be aware of the limitations of the printing process that mean a 'hairline' (a default setting that is sometimes as thin as 0.125pt) is often too fine to print. The diagram below shows some potential line weight printing problems.

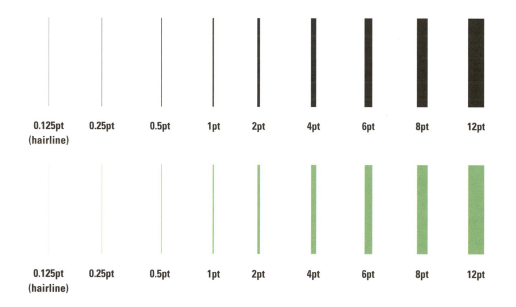

**process lines**
Producing a line in a solid process colour generally provides an accurate print. Here even a hairline setting produces a solid, visible line.

**CMYK**
Printing lines in a mixed-percentage colour is less accurate as two screens are used to produce the colour featuring half-tone dots at different sizes. Aligning these dots in a line such as an arrow causes visible problems.

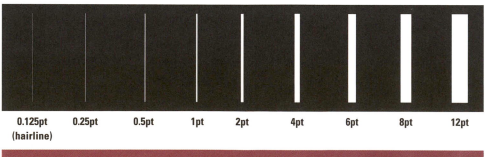

**reversing out of a process colour**
Reversing a line out of a solid process colour produces good results, but may have problems with fine lines due to dot gain.

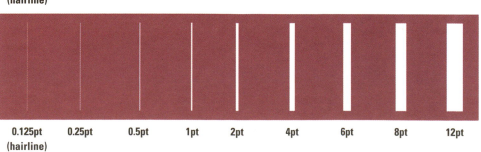

**reversing out of CMYK**
Reversing lines out of CMYK is less accurate due to potential colour registration problems. For this reason fine lines can be difficult to produce in reverse.

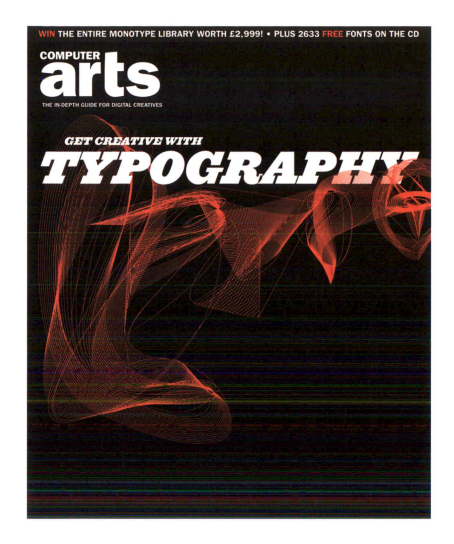

WIN THE ENTIRE MONOTYPE LIBRARY WORTH £2,999! • PLUS 2633 FREE FONTS ON THE CD

**COMPUTER**
**arts**
THE IN-DEPTH GUIDE FOR DIGITAL CREATIVES

*GET CREATIVE WITH*
**TYPOGRAPHY**

### 'Computer Arts' (left)

Pictured is the cover of *Computer Arts* magazine created by Research Studios. It features a design that uses vector graphic lines to produce the word type. Due to the fineness of some of these lines, this was printed in a special process colour.

### London Calling (below)

This logo was created by Social Design and features the use of concentric rules of decreasing line weights to build up the letters within it.

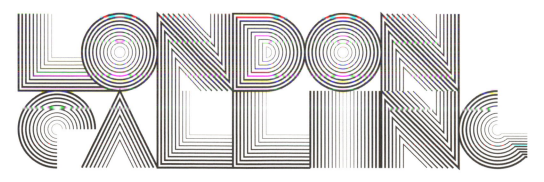

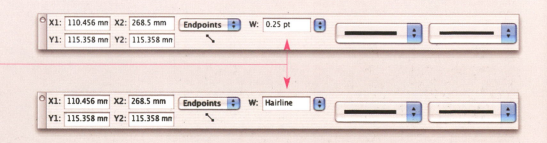

### being specific

A designer can insert a specific measurement for a hairline (top) rather than allow it to be an ambiguous measurement (bottom), as these command boxes show. How thick is a hairline? If you're not sure then you shouldn't be specifying it.

# print processes

Printing is a process that applies ink or varnish from a printing plate to a substrate through the application of pressure. Modern printing technology also includes inkjet printing whereby the ink is sprayed on to the substrate.

## printing methods

There are four main processes used by the commercial printing industry – offset lithography, gravure, letterpress and silk screen – all of which differ in cost, production quality and production rate or volume.

### lithography

Lithographic printing is a process through which the inked image from a printing plate is transferred or offset on to a rubber blanket roller, which is then pressed against the substrate. Lithography uses a smooth printing plate and functions on the basis that oil and water repel each other. When the plate passes under the ink roller, non-image areas that have a water film repel the oily inks that stick to the image areas.

Lithography produces good photographic reproduction and fine linework on a variety of stocks. The printing plates are easy to prepare and high speeds are achievable, which helps make it a low-cost printing method.

Offset lithography is available in sheet-fed printing presses and continuous web presses. Sheet-fed presses are used for lower production runs such as flyers, brochures and magazines, while web printing is used for high-volume print jobs such as newspapers, magazines and reports.

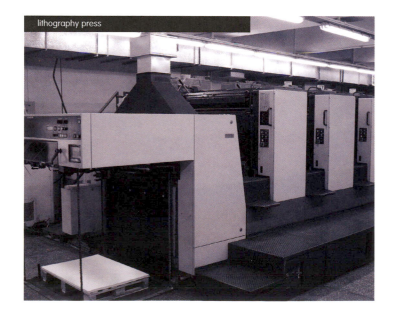

lithography press

yellow ink reservoir on offset printing press

## web printing

Web printing uses stock that is supplied on massive rolls rather than individual sheets. This allows for higher volume printing speeds and a lower production cost per unit for high-volume print jobs. Webs can be used with lithography, but more commonly with relief printing methods such as rotogravure and flexography as the plates are more durable. Due to the scale and cost of this production method, it is not suitable for low-volume print runs.

**different printing applications will require different half-tone screens:**

(Higher quality printing uses finer screen values)

| Printing method | Lines per inch |
| --- | --- |
| Newsprint | 85–110 |
| Web offset | 133 |
| Standard sheet-fed offset | 150 |
| Fine quality | 175–200 |

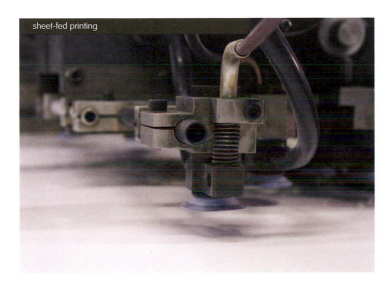
sheet-fed printing

paper roll on web printing press

## common problems with web and litho printing

The main drawbacks to offset lithography concern print run, as the cost benefits of the method are achieved with medium to long print runs. However, for high or very high print runs image quality can start to suffer due to wear on the plate, so rotogravure is generally used instead.

Colour control can be an issue due to problems with the ink/water balance on the plate and the presence of water can cause more absorbent substrates to distort. A dense ink film is also difficult to achieve.

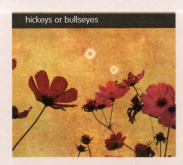
hickeys or bullseyes

mis-registration

setoff

colour variation

Spots or other imperfections on the printed image caused by dried ink, dirt or other particles on the press can cause hickeys or bullseyes such as these above the flowers.

The misalignment of one or more of the printed images, perhaps due to the presence of water in the lithographic process, that can distort the stock. Here mis-registration is noticeable by the blocks of yellow and red colour.

Also called offset, this problem sees ink from one printed sheet unintentionally mark or transfer to the next sheet, such as the smudge over this woman's face.

Failure to maintain a constant and adequate ink/water balance on the printing plate can result in colour variation, particularly over a long print run, which has caused banding in the landscape above.

moveable type

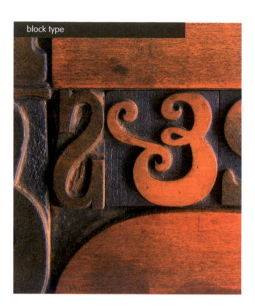

block type

**Tokyo Type Directors Club (above)**
This is a poster for an exhibition at the Tokyo Type Directors Club produced in association with John Warwicker from Tomato design studio in London that was produced using letterpress type.

### letterpress

A method of relief printing whereby an inked, raised surface is pressed against a substrate. Letterpress was the first commercial printing method and the source of many printing methods. The raised surface that is inked for printing may be made from single type blocks, cast lines or engraved plates. Relief printing methods can be identified by the sharp and precise edges to letters and their heavier ink borders.

Rotogravure is a more common commercial relief print process in which an image is engraved into a copper printing plate that is pressed directly against the substrate. Using a laser or diamond tool, small cells are engraved into the plate to hold the ink that will transfer to the stock, with a separate printing unit for each colour. Rotogravure is a high speed printing process that can give the highest production volume and has the widest printing presses. Rotogravure is used for very large print runs.

Another method with which the image is carried by surface differences in the plate is flexography. This process creates a rubber relief of the image, which is inked and pressed against the substrate. Developed for printing packaging materials, the process was traditionally a lower quality reproduction method, but it now competes with rotogravure and lithography, particularly as it can print on a wider range of substrates due to the flexibility of its plate. Flexography is used for medium to large print runs.

Both rotogravure and flexography tend to use lower viscosity inks than lithography, allowing for faster drying times.

**Forme London calling cards (below)**
These calling cards were created by and for Forme London print studio. They feature fonts from its letterpress archive and the words 'comp' and 'spools' refer to two terms frequently used in letterpress printing methods. A spool is used to collect type in a monotype keyboard, while comp is an abbreviation of compositor, the person that composes type to put on a page.

**Levi's (below)**
This design, created by Kate Gibb and Rob Petrie for Levi's, features a tritone produced using a screen print to colour different sections and highlight the clothing.

ink is applied to the screen that contains the image

ink is drawn through the screen and on to the substrate

the finished print job

## screen-printing
Screen-printing is a relatively low-volume printing method in which a viscous ink is passed through a screen – originally made from silk – that holds a design, on to a substrate. Although a relatively slow, low-volume and expensive printing method, screen-printing allows images to be applied to a wide range of substrates, including cloth, ceramics and metals, which are beyond the pale of other printing methods. The viscous inks allow specific colours to be applied and can also be used to create a raised surface that adds a tactile element to a design.

**Wedding stationery (above)**
Pictured above is a screen-printer printing wedding stationery that was created by The Gentle Group design studio.

# on-press

Colour can be adjusted on a printing press while a job is printing. This is normally done to achieve colour consistency or to correct any colour defects that arise during the printing process.

## adjusting colour

Colour adjustments may be made on-press to account for colour variation caused by changes in ink density or plate pressure. A printer makes colour adjustments to ensure that the colours printing are the same as those on the colour proof that is used as a reference and/or contract proof.

### proof marking

A designer often needs to review a wet proof of a job and mark up where changes to the colour are necessary. A designer or printer uses an eye glass to check colour production against the control strips and uses the symbols below to accurately specify the changes required to print colour, such as increasing or decreasing the intensity of the hue.

### colour checking, basic tools

To check the colour of a job a printed sheet is pulled from the press and checked using a colour densitometer, a device that uses a light source and a photoelectric cell to measure optical density, or a spectrophotometer. The measurements obtained can be compared with those obtained from the colour proof, a test strip, or a Pantone colour swatch when special colours are printed. A printer also uses a loupe or eyeglass to check colour registration.

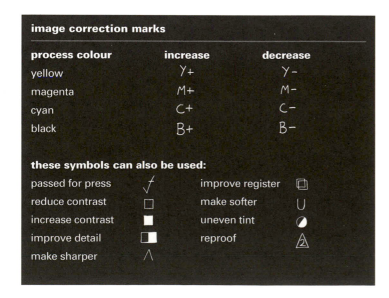

**image correction marks**

| process colour | increase | decrease |
|---|---|---|
| yellow | Y+ | Y− |
| magenta | M+ | M− |
| cyan | C+ | C− |
| black | B+ | B− |

**these symbols can also be used:**

| | | | |
|---|---|---|---|
| passed for press | √ | improve register | ◰ |
| reduce contrast | ☐ | make softer | U |
| increase contrast | ◼ | uneven tint | ◑ |
| improve detail | ◧ | reproof | ⚠ |
| make sharper | ∧ | | |

densitometer

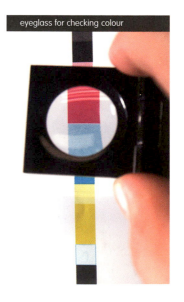

eyeglass for checking colour

four colours overprint · yellow · tint of magenta · star target · cyan + yellow · cyan · magenta + yellow

## striker bar

A printed sheet has a striker bar containing a series of predefined colours printed along its edge for colour checking. The bar includes additive primaries, subtractive primaries and overprints, as shown above, while star targets allow a printer to test for dot gain. Even though a densitometer may say a job is printing accurately, whether a job needs more or less colour running is a judgement that requires human instinct.

## the press

A modern lithographic printing press can control the colour density/plate pressure on the stock, which allows a printer to adjust in increments the balance of each colour being printed. A printer regularly pulls sheets from the press during printing to check against the colour proof. Readjustments can be made if necessary by using the controls (below left) that change ink flow of different vertical slithers directly on to the stock. The example below has an exaggerated colour alteration of a single slither to show how an alteration affects all the pages it prints.

## the imposed sheet

The way a sheet is imposed affects how much colour can be altered while printing. In the example below, eight pages are printed to view, which means that altering a vertical strip on a lower page will have an impact on a higher page. When all colours are similar, this is not usually problematic. However, isolated patches of solid colour, such as a black square, can be more difficult to alter. Running a bouncer behind the colour can reduce this problem, as it would use two colours, meaning that any individual colour has to do less work.

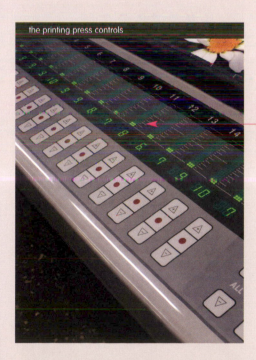

the printing press controls

A designer may be able to plan a publication to group strong colours together in vertical slithers, such as the black in the example, so alterations to the colour are applied to the whole slither. However, it is more common to find a solid colour above a very light page that minimises the amount that one colour can be pushed, which is why colour correction issues must be resolved at the proofing stage (see page 138) before going to press. Bending a colour to remove a cast will alter the colour reproduction of other elements on the printed sheet, which needs to be borne in mind as many jobs are printed with eight or 16 pages to view.

# paper

A designer can choose from a wide range of stocks on which to print a job. Stocks differ by size, colour, texture, composition, printability and various other factors that need to be taken into account during the selection process.

## paper qualities

GSM, grain and paper direction are key physical characteristics to consider when selecting and using a stock for a publication.

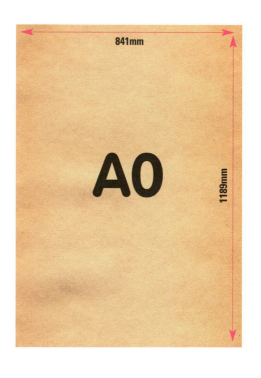

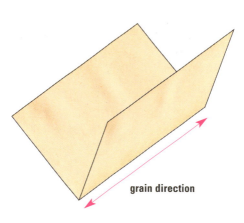

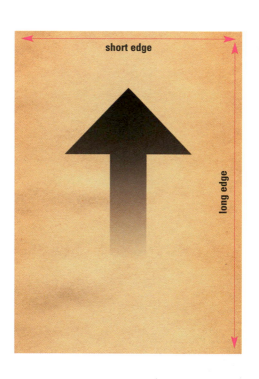

### GSM
GSM (or grams per square metre) is a weight measurement that is part of a paper specification based on the weight of a square metre of the stock. The higher the GSM value, the more weighty a stock feels. An A0 page is equal to one metre square, meaning that grams per square metre equates to the weight of a single A0 sheet.

### paper grain
Paper produced on a paper machine has a grain because the fibres from which it is made line up during the manufacturing process in the direction that it passes through the paper-making machine. The grain is the direction in which most of the fibres lay. This characteristic means that paper is easier to fold, bend or tear along its grain direction.

### direction
The direction of fibres in paper for laser printers, such as those found in offices, typically has a grain that runs parallel to the long side of the paper to allow it to pass more easily through the printer.

**'Understanding Italian Wine' (left)**
This book was created by Social Design for vinter Enotria Winecellars and is produced on an uncoated stock so that the reader experiences its tactile qualities. Lacking the brilliance that a coated stock gives to colours, the publication has a softer and more natural feel and look.

**'Millennium' (below)**
This book, created by Studio Thomson, features a foil-stamped, red leatherette cover stock, to provide a facsimile of the look and feel of a bible.

**life lasting pr (above left)**
A business card from identity, designed by Parent Design. This features a deep foil imprinted into grey board stock, creating a contrast between the tactile quality of the stock and the smooth impression of the foil.

**Prestigious Textiles (left)**
This is the cover of a brochure created by Social Design for fabric supplier, PT. It features an embossed and patterned cover stock that mimics the tactile feel of cloth.

## paper types and print quality

Many different types of paper stock are available to the designer. For example, this book prints on four different stocks: woodfree is the main stock used, a matt art (pages 33–48), gloss art (pages 65–80) and a coloured woodfree (pages 161–176). In addition to adding different colours and textures to a print job, these also have different printability characteristics and cost. Paper characteristics that affect printability include its smoothness, absorbency, opacity and ink holdout. The table opposite is designed as a quick guide to the characteristics of some main paper types.

### smoothness
The smooth surface of these stocks is obtained through the use of filler elements that may be polished with calendering rollers. They are typically glossy as well.

### absorbency
Stocks have different absorbency levels, which is the degree to which the ink penetrates it. Printing inks tend to dry quicker on absorbent stocks, but absorbency may cause problems such as dot gain.

### opacity
Opacity is used to describe the extent to which whatever is printed on one side of a sheet shows through and is visible on the other. High-opacity papers have no show-through.

### ink holdout
This is the degree to which a stock resists ink penetration due to its relative lack of absorbency. Coated stocks may be particularly prone to ink holdout as the ink sits on the surface, which in turn increases drying time.

**John Robertson Architects (above)**
This three-part purchase order for John Robertson Architects features the use of NCR paper in three coloured stocks.

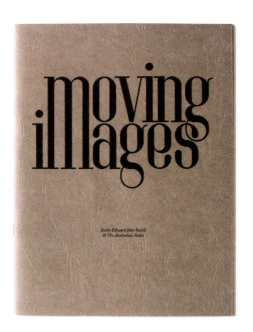

**'Moving Images' (above)**
This brochure cover, created by 3 Deep Design, features the understated beauty of a textured stock with a simple print.

**'Rude' (above)**
This cover for Rude was created by Third Eye Design and is printed on plike, which gives a synthetic, futuristic rubbery feel.

| type of paper | notes | primary uses | secondary uses | effect |
|---|---|---|---|---|
| Antique | A high-quality paper with a clay coating on both sides to give a good printing surface, especially for half-tones, where definition and detail are important. | To add texture to publications such as annual reports. | Stationery and flyers. | A textured stock with a rough or matt surface. |
| Art | A high-quality paper with a clay coating on both sides to give a good printing surface, especially for half-tones, where definition and detail are important. | Colour printing and magazines. | Flyers, calendars and brochures. | A glossy, high brightness surface that is smooth to the touch. |
| Artboard | Uncoated board. | Cover stock. | Flyers and packaging. | A stiff stock. |
| Cartridge | A thick white paper. Ink and pencil drawings are particularly well produced on this. | Stationery and annual reports. | Mail shots. | A stiff feel, available in several colours. |
| Cast coated | Wet-coated paper is pressed (cast) against a hot, polished metal drum to obtain a high gloss. | Magazines and brochures. | Promotional material. | A smooth, glossy surface. |
| Chromo | A waterproof coating is applied to one side of the paper to allow for embossing and varnishing processes. | Labels, wrappings and covers. | Applications where only one side has to be printed. | Clay coated on one side; can be glossy or matt. |
| Flock | Paper coated with flock; very fine woollen surface. Used for decorative covers. Other coatings might be refuse or vegetable fibre dust to give a velvety or cloth-like appearance. | Decorative covers. | Packaging. | A textured, decorative surface. |
| Greyboard | Lined or unlined board made from waste paper. Packaging material. | Packaging material. | Covers. | Rough texture, good bulk and grey colour. |
| Mechanical | Produced using wood pulp and acidic chemicals, this paper is suitable for short term use as it yellows and fades quickly. | Newspapers and directories. | Magazines, inserts, flyers, coupons and books. | Higher brightness and smoothness than newsprint, but uncoated and matt. |
| NCR (No Carbon Required) | A carbonless coating to make duplicate copies. Available in two- to six-part. | Forms and purchase orders. | Receipts. | The application of pressure produces an impression on subsequent parts. |
| Newsprint | Made primarily of mechanically-ground wood pulp, this is the cheapest paper that can withstand standard printing processes. It has a short life-span and reproduces colour poorly. | Newspapers and comics. | Low-quality printing. | Absorbent, comparatively rough surface. |
| Plike | A rubberised substrate. | Cover stock. | Flyers. | Rubbery texture. |
| Uncoated woodfree | This paper is the most commonly used in non-commercial printing. Most stationery and printer/photocopier paper falls into this category, although some offset grades are also used for general commercial printing. | Office paper (printer and photocopy paper, stationery). | Forms and envelopes. | A white paper with a slightly rough, non-glossy surface. |

# sustainability

Environmental sustainability is becoming a key concern for both clients and final consumers in order to reduce the impact of production and our lifestyles on the Earth's resources. Companies are now actively engaging in efforts to reduce their environmental impact by reducing the use of resources and changing purchasing habits to utilise products that are less harmful than their substitutes.

## sustainable printing

For several years now, sustainable printing has been a growing concept in the printing industry and many printers specialise in offering environmentally friendly services to cater for this growing niche of consumers that want to make a difference.

This effort goes beyond the use of recycled paper to include developments such as chlorine-free paper, 'waterless' technology (to avoid the use of isopropanol alcohol, one of the printing industry's major pollutants), and environmentally-friendly inks made from linseed and soya vegetable oils (to replace traditional printing inks). Vegetable inks are less toxic and easier to remove than traditional pigment transfer vehicles, which eases the deinking process during paper recycling, according to The National Non-Food Crops Centre.

Graphic designers have a huge role to play in this change in behaviour, as they typically specify the print job. Design Anarchy details simple changes that designers can make to reduce the environmental impact of printing. These include reducing point size, sending PDFs instead of print-outs and obtaining print estimates at the start of a job where there may be cost-saving flexibility related to format size.

Print customers can do their part in many ways by specifying the use of recycled and/or environmentally-friendly products, but also by providing more precise job specifications, such as giving a more accurate print run to avoid the need to dispose of thousands of overs, using smaller formats and extents, and minimising the use of foils, varnishes, specials and other treatments such as die cutting that perhaps have higher resource usage.

An environmental consciousness is often thought to imply a trade-off in terms of (visual) quality, which many print industry clients are not prepared to accept. However, many environmentally friendly products and technologies produce high quality results, and it is worth remembering how recycled paper has evolved from a poor quality product to something much better today.

## environment ISO 14000 accredited

ISO 14000 is an international standard that certifies that a company follows environmental management standards to minimise the negative impact its operations have on the environment, in addition to compliance with all relevant local and international legislation.

### 'World' (left)

Pictured is *World*, a publication reporting on developments in science, engineering, architecture, business and politics that was created by Sagmeister Inc. for publisher Harry N Abrams Inc. It features a die-cut slipcase that will change colour over time if left in direct light.

**'Frost*' (above)**
The new mini *Frost** book, produced by Frost* Design, Sydney, showcases work in progress from its first year in business and is printed with vegetable inks.

**FSC (right)**
The Forest Stewardship Council logo. This non-profit organisation looks for solutions to the problems created by bad forestry practices. Paper produced from forests managed in accordance to the principles of the FSC can be endorsed with this logo to indicate that it has been produced responsibly, thus allowing paper buyers to make a more informed choice when selecting stocks.

FSC

# chapter six
# finishing

Finishing includes a wide range of processes to provide the finishing touches to a design once the substrate has been printed. These processes include die cutting, binding, special print techniques, laminates, varnishes, folding, foil blocking and screen-printing, all of which can transform an ordinary-looking piece into something much more interesting and dynamic.

Finishing processes can add decorative elements to a printed piece, such as the shimmer of a foil block or the texture of an emboss. They can also provide added functionality to a design and even be a constituent part of a publication's format, for example, a matt lamination protects a substrate, making it last longer.

Although the application of print-finishing techniques signals the end of the production process, these techniques should not be considered as afterthoughts, but as an integral part of a design at the planning stage.

**'The Arts and Crafts Movement'
(facing page)**
This book cover was created by Webb &
Webb design studio for publisher, Phaidon.
It features a deep emboss of a design by
Victorian fabric designer, William Morris, for
Windrush wallpaper.

PHAIDON

# binding

Binding is a process through which the various pages that comprise a job are gathered and securely held together so that they function as a publication.

## types of binding

Many different types of binding are available and they all have different durability, aesthetics, costs and functional characteristics, as shown on the opposite page.

**Douglas Gordon (below)**
This box was created for an exhibition by Douglas Gordon at the Guggenheim Museum, Berlin, by Sagmeister Inc. design studio. It contains postcards featuring works in the exhibition and thus acts as an informal binding for them. It also contains a mirror that reflects the word 'vanity' as a reference to the mirror-hopping practised by those that are over concerned about their appearance.

The binding method chosen for a publication can add to the narrative of the information it contains. For example, a case binding lends a more formal tone to a work while a perfect binding is more informal and disposable.

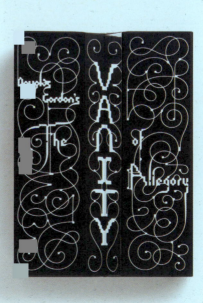

**comb binding**
A spine (comb) of plastic rings that bind and allow a document to open flat.

**spiral binding**
A spiral of metal wire that winds through punched holes allowing the publication to open flat.

**wiro binding**
A spine of metal (wiro) rings that bind and allow a document to open flat.

**open bind**
A book bound without a cover to leave an exposed spine.

**belly band**
A printed band that wraps around a publication, typically used with magazines.

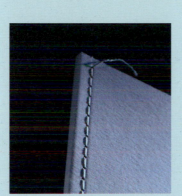

**singer stitch**
A binding method whereby the pages are sewn together with one continual thread.

**elastic bands**
An informal binding whereby an elastic band holds the pages together and nestles in the centre fold.

**clips and bolts**
A fastening device that holds loose pages together. This usually requires the insertion of a punched or drilled hole for the bolt or clip to pass through.

**perfect bound**
The backs of sections are removed and held together with a flexible adhesive, which also attaches a paper cover to the spine, and the fore edge trimmed flat. Commonly used for paperback books.

**case or edition binding**
A common hard cover bookbinding method that sews signatures together, flattens the spine, applies endsheets and head and tailbands to the spine. Hard covers are attached, the spine is usually rounded and grooves along the cover edge act as hinges.

**Canadian**
A wiro-bound publication with a wrap-around cover and an enclosed spine. A complete wrap-around cover is a full Canadian and a partial wrap-around is a half Canadian.

**saddle stitch**
Signatures are nested and bound with wire stitches, applied through the spine along the centrefold.

## bookbinding

Bookbinding involves a variety of processes to produce a finished book. The various sections that form the book block are either stitched or glued to hold them together. The book block may then be shaped or curved.

End papers of stronger stock are added to provide material for the cover to adhere to, and headbands and tailbands are added to provide protection to the top and bottom of the binding, as well as for decorative effect. Finally, the cover is applied.

**head and tailbands**
Head and tailbands can be patterned or coloured, depending upon the fabric selected.

**text block**
The text block or book block is comprised of the printed signatures or sections that will form the pages of the publication.

**bulk**
The dust jacket spine measurement needs to take into account the book block bulk, which depends upon the number of signatures, with the addition of 3mm for the boards. As a rule, the spine will measure whatever the bulking dummy measures, plus an additional 6–7mm.

**flaps**
Flaps are an extension of the cover or dust jacket, which fold back and into the publication. These usually carry information about the author, a synopsis on the work, or other information, and can be any size in theory, although 75mm is considered optimum for a dust jacket to grip the book.

**end pages**
These are the pages that secure the text block to the boards of the cover. They are typically made from a strong stock such as cartridge paper. They may also be printed to add a visual element to the inside cover.

**ribbon**
A ribbon may also be attached to the headband to be used as a page marker.

## a note on spine orientation

Spine text can be orientated to read top to bottom or bottom to top. In Europe, the standard is usually to read bottom to top, such as in the example far right, created by Research Studios. In the UK, however, spine text usually reads top to bottom so that when a book is laid on a table both the spine and the cover are readable, such as in the example right, created by Social Design. This alignment is also easier for most people to read when publications are kept in a bookcase. Spine text can also be printed horizontally although this usually occurs on larger, wider volumes that provide a broader measure.

Here, the spine text reads top to bottom, allowing it to be read together with the cover.

Here, the spine text reads bottom to top.

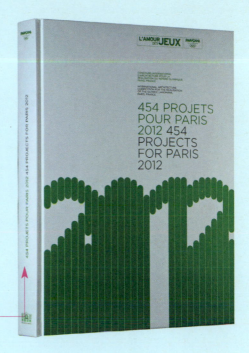

## z-bind

A z-bind features a 'z'-shaped cover which is used to join two separate text blocks, typically with both sections having a perfect bind. This provides a clear yet functional way of separating different types of content. However, with large publications this can become unwieldy if the cover stock is not sufficiently robust to support the weight of the pages.

### dual bindings

Some publications feature dual bindings where two or more separate book blocks are united into one publication, such as the z-bind used below.

### Clarity Motor Yachts (below, left)

A brochure for Clarity Motor Yachts, created by Parent Design. This features a z-bind to separate information about the two distinct areas of its business: private charter and corporate events.

### Orange (below)

This publication, produced by Thirteen for the pension plan of mobile telecommunications company, Orange, features a z-bind to separate the two distinct information elements it contains.

# special techniques

A range of techniques, such as speciality printing, give a designer the possibility of adding an extra touch of value-adding excitement to a design.

### speciality printing

A number of print techniques allow a designer to produce something different to what standard offset lithography can produce. These techniques may be more expensive due to the additional set-up time required and lower volumes they can produce, but they certainly add value to a design.

**Monsters Ink (above)**
Pictured above are invites to a Halloween party, created by and for NB: Studio. They feature illustrations of monsters by James Graham that were screen-printed in luminous ink on to black stock to give a dark, contrasting feel to the piece that glows in the dark.

**Somerset House invite (above right)**
Pictured is an invite that features a matt orange foil block on duplexed stock, which creates a slight deboss and tactile element. Foils are usually bright, but matt foils add a subtle quality to a job.

**Minera Santa Barbara business card (right)**
Pictured is a business card designed by the owner of Chilean iron ore producer Santa Barbara that features a design laser-cut into steel and filled with ink to leave a memorable impression.

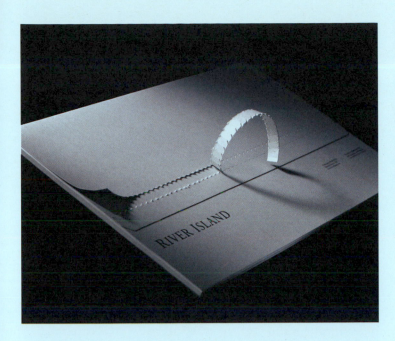

**perforation**

Perforation, or perf cutting, is a process that creates a cut-out area in a substrate to weaken it so that it can be detached, or it is used to create a decorative effect. Pictured above is a mailout package created by Third Eye Design for fashion retailer River Island, which features perforated stock.

**duplexing**

Duplexing is the bonding of two stocks to form a single substrate with different colours or textures on each side. Pictured above is an invite created by SEA for paper merchant GF Smith, which features a duplexed substrate to highlight two of the client's paper stocks.

**foils**

Foil blocking is a process whereby a coloured foil is pressed on to a substrate via a heated die. Also called foil stamp, heat stamp or foil emboss, the process allows a designer to add a shiny finish to specific design elements such as title text. Pictured above is a cover submission design for Project Perfection, created by Gavin Ambrose.

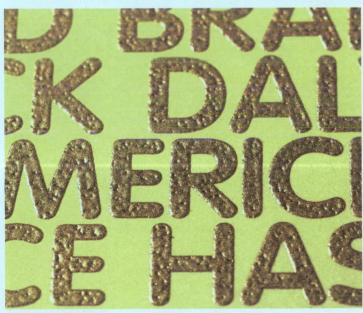

**thermography**

Thermography is a print-finishing process that produces raised lettering by fusing thermographic powder to a design in an oven. Pictured above is a Christmas card created by design studio SEA for the Lisa Pritchard Agency. The text has been thermographically printed to give the letters a raised, bubbly, mottled surface that is highly visible and very tactile.

## embossing and debossing

An emboss or deboss is a design that is stamped into a substrate to produce a decorative raised or indented surface respectively.

### embossing

An emboss uses a magnesium, copper or brass die holding an image to stamp the stock and leave an impression. As the design has to push through the stock, designs are usually slightly oversized, with heavier lines and extra space inserted between the letters in a word. Copper and brass are more durable die materials than magnesium and so should be used for high print run jobs, those using thick or abrasive stocks and those where the design is more detailed.

Thinner stocks can hold more detail than thicker stocks, but intricate designs do not reproduce well. Thicker stocks generally require thicker lines to reproduce well as the image has to press through more fibres. Soft papers are easier to emboss and coated stocks hold detail well, but the coating may crack, meaning that uncoated stock is better for deep embossing. An emboss may be made with foil to give colouration to the design, but they are frequently made blind without the use of foil to add a tactile element to a design.

### Feeder (right)

Pictured is Feeder's *Picture of Perfect Youth*, a CD package created by Social Design. It features a gold foil block cover for the title text. Foil blocking is a form of deboss in that the design is stamped in metallic foil into the substrate, creating a slight recess that holds the foil. Foil blocking adds value to a design by giving it an additional tactile quality and a visually attractive, shiny metallic finish.

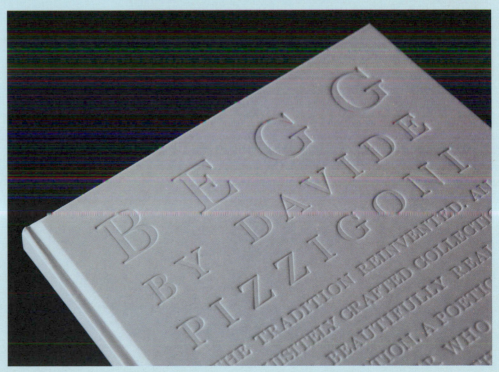

**'Lost History' (above)**
*Lost History 2007* is a catalogue created by Third Eye Design for fashion label, Timberland. It features a four-colour cover with a deep emboss to add a subtle, tactile element.

**River Island (above right)**
This brochure was designed by Third Eye Design for fashion retailer, River Island. It features a deep cover emboss that juxtaposes with the raised texture of the singer-sewn binding.

**BEGG (right)**
A brochure created by Third Eye Design for Scottish cashmere manufacturer BEGG that features a deep emboss into a white cover stock. The typeface characters appear as though they have been carved in marble due to the white-on-white effect produced, which is timeless and elegant.

**debossing**
A deboss uses a metal dye containing a design, which is stamped from above on to stock to leave an indentation. Debossing also produces better results on thicker stock because a deeper indentation is achieved.

The ability of an emboss or deboss to leave a good impression is a function of the fineness of the design and the stock calliper. Thinner stocks can hold finer lines, but there is a danger of puncturing the stock. Thicker stocks are more robust, but lose fine detail as the design presses through more paper fibres.

# cutting methods

Die, laser and kiss cutting are all methods for removing portions of stock to create different shapes.

### die cutting

Die cutting uses a steel die to cut away a specified section of a design. It is mainly used to add a decorative element to a print job and enhance the visual performance of the piece.

**Peter and Paul (left)**

This business card was created by and for Peter and Paul design studio. The card is used by both Peter and Paul as it features the name of one partner on one side and the other on the reverse. Additional information is embossed into the mottled black stock to create a tactile and memorable identity.

**award mailer (right)**

A mailer, created by NB: Studio, containing information about an award it has received. The card is die cut in the shape of a bird, with the text starting with: 'A little bird told me...'

A little bird told me that NB: Studio have won the Benchmarks retail award for their branding work with Mothercare. And they were runner up for the 'Best of Show' award too. You can find out more at www.nbstudio.co.uk/mothercare

**Somerset House (right)**

These images are taken from a rebranding exercise for Somerset House in London, created by Research Studios. The new identity features a logo with cut-out stencil text based on the rectangular outline of the Somerset House site as seen from the air.

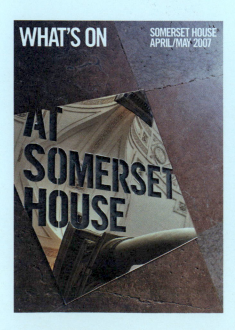

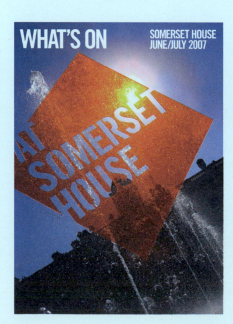

## laser cutting

Laser cutting uses a laser to cut shapes into the stock rather than use a metal tool. Laser cutting can produce more intricate cut-outs with a cleaner edge than a steel die although the heat of the laser burns the cut edge. Faster set-up times mean faster job turnaround.

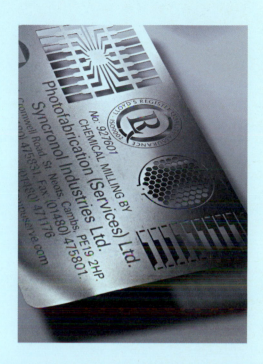

### Hugo Boss (left)

Pictured is a laser-cut typographic cover for the Guggenheim Hugo Boss art prize in New York designed by Sarah Noellenheidt and Matthias Ernstberger, with art direction by Stefan Sagmeister. The artist pages were designed by the nominees themselves.

### laser-etched card (right)

Pictured is a laser-cut and etched business card for Syncronol Industries Ltd. that demonstrates the accuracy of its fabrication techniques. The detail of the etching can be seen in the intricate honeycomb pattern.

## kiss cutting

This is a die cutting method often used with self-adhesive substrates, whereby the face stock is die cut but not its backing sheet, to facilitate the easy removal of the cut stock. Kiss cutting is commonly seen in the production of stickers. The artwork supplied for kiss cutting needs to include a cutter guide as shown below right. A common form of kiss cut is called Crack-Back, which is a brand produced by Fasson.

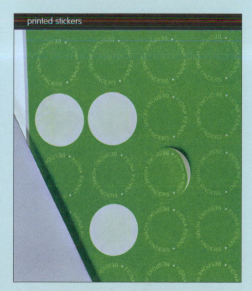

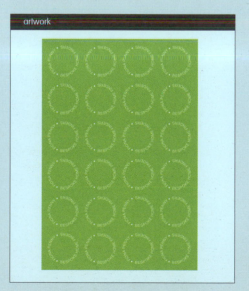

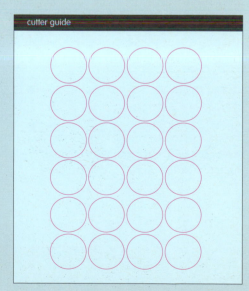

These stickers were produced using a kiss-cut die cut.

This is the artwork that was used to produce the stickers.

This is the cutter guide supplied with this kiss-cut job.

# laminates and varnishes

Laminates and varnishes are print finishes applied to the printed job to add a finishing touch to the surface.

## laminate types

A laminate is a layer of plastic coating that is heat-sealed on to the stock to produce a smooth and impervious finish and to provide a protective layer to cover stock. A varnish is a colourless coating, applied to a printed piece to protect it from wear or smudging, and to enhance the visual appearance of the design or elements within it, such as a spot varnish.

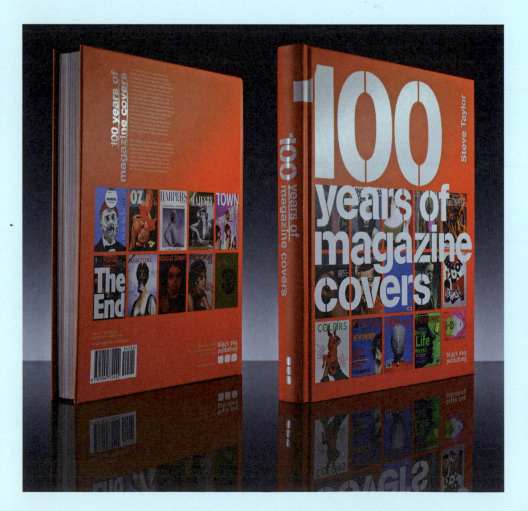

**Somerset House invite (above)**
Pictured is a perforated, concertina invite created by Gavin Ambrose and highlighting the activities of a new learning centre at Somerset House. Each panel is coated in a gloss varnish, adding reflectivity to the piece and also increasing durability.

**'100 Years of Magazine Covers' (left)**
Pictured is *100 Years of Magazine Covers*, a book written by Steve Taylor and designed by Research Studios for Black Dog Publishing. It features a spot UV gloss on the cover and round-back binding to add a special touch.

Pictured above is a schematic of the artwork that is to receive a varnish.

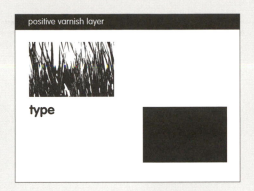

This image shows the file for a positive varnish application in which the images will receive the varnish (the grass stalks).

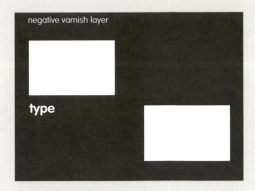

This image shows the negative varnish file in which the non-image areas will receive the varnish and the pictures will remain untouched.

## supplying artwork for a laminate or varnish

Any part of a printed surface can have a spot varnish or laminate applied. To achieve this, a designer must send a separate file to show exactly where it will be placed. The file contains the artwork with the spot varnish or laminate design presented in black as it will run as a solid colour without any screening, while all other areas are white. Varnishes and laminates can be applied in different ways to produce a variety of effects.

For example, a positive varnish could be applied to the page above to cover the text and images. Conversely, a negative varnish could be applied where there are unprinted areas. Varnish can be used to enhance elements printed on to a matt stock. If printing on a high gloss stock, the application of a matt varnish would take the sheen off the selected areas, subduing them and allowing the unvarnished area to shine and be the focal point. Remember that everything black will be varnished or laminated and everything white will not be.

## types of varnish

### gloss

Colours appear richer and more vivid when printed with a gloss varnish, so photographs appear sharper and more saturated. For this reason, a gloss finish is often used for brochures or other photographic publications.

### matt (or dull)

The opposite of a gloss varnish, a matt coating will soften the appearance of a printed image. It will also make text easier to read as it diffuses light, thus reducing glare.

### neutral

The application of a basic, almost invisible, coating that seals the printing ink without affecting the appearance of the job. It is often used to accelerate the drying of fast turnaround print jobs (such as leaflets) on matt and satin papers, on which inks dry more slowly.

### pearlescent

A varnish that subtly reflects myriad colours to give a luxurious effect.

### satin (or silk)

This coating tends to represent a midway point between gloss and matt varnishes.

### textured spot UV

Textures can be applied to a design through the use of a spot UV. The textures that can be obtained are sandpaper, leather, crocodile skin and raised.

### UV varnish

An ultraviolet varnish can be applied to printed paper and dried by exposure to UV radiation in order to create a coating that is glossier than any other. A printed page with this varnish will feel shiny and slightly sticky. UV varnish can be applied all over a publication (**full-bleed UV**) or to certain parts of a design (**spot UV**).

## types of laminate

### matt

A matt laminate helps diffuse light and reduce glare to increase the readability of text-heavy designs.

### satin

This laminate provides a finish that is between matt and gloss. It provides some highlight, but is not as flat as matt.

### gloss

A highly reflective laminate that is used to enhance the appearance of graphic elements and photographs on covers as it increases colour saturation.

### sand

A laminate that creates a subtle sand grain within a design.

### leather

A laminate that gives a subtle leather texture to a design.

# folding and trimming

Folding encompasses a range of different methods for turning a printed sheet into a more compact form or signature.

## types of fold

The majority of folding techniques make use of the basic valley and mountain folds to create a series of peaks and troughs.

### valley fold
Held horizontally, a valley fold has a central crease at the bottom with the panels rising upwards to form the sides.

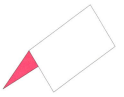

### mountain fold
Held horizontally, a mountain fold has a central crease at the top with the panels falling downwards.

**The George Hotel & Brasserie brochure (above)**
This mailer, produced by Gavin Ambrose for The George Hotel & Brasserie, features a cover that is a few millimetres larger than the signature and the first fold also has an edge that is slightly larger so that there is no possibility of the second panel showing.

**Orange hot desk signs (above)**
These tent cards, created by Thirteen for Orange, feature two parallel folds and adhesive to create a prism shape. The cards, printed on both sides, can be reversed to indicate a member of staff is either 'in' or 'out'.

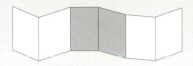  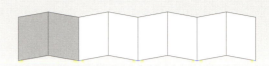 

**front / back accordion fold** With three parallel folds, the two-panel outer wings fold into and out of the centre. The double-panel centre serves as the cover.

**harmonica self-cover folder** An accordion fold where the first two panels form a cover that the other panels fold into. The first two panels need to be larger than the others to allow for creep.

  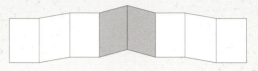 

**mock book fold** Essentially an accordion fold where the penultimate two panels form a cover that the other panels fold into to create a book.

**double gatefold** The gatefold has three panels that fold in towards the centre of the publication.

**front / back gatefold** An extra double panel that folds inside the front and / or back panel.

**incline tab** The stock top is cut away at an incline and accordion folded to present panels of increasing size from front to back.

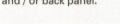    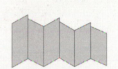 

**triple parallel fold** Parallel folds creating a section that nests within the cover panels with a front opening. May be used for maps.

**tab fold** The stock top is cut away horizontally and accordion folded so that each pair of panels decreases in size from the full-size panel.

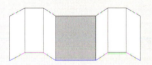    

**back / front folder** Wings either side of the central panel have a double parallel fold so that they can fold around and cover both sides of the central panel.

**ascending folder** The stock is accordion folded with increasing widths between folds so that each panel increases in size from front to back.

**half cover from behind** An accordion fold where the penultimate panel forms a back cover that the other panels fold into to create a book, but the half-size end panel folds around the book from behind to cover the front, together with the half-size first panel.

**staggered folder design** Stock is cut away horizontally from top and bottom to make each successive panel smaller than its predecessor and accordion folded.

 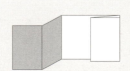  

**duelling z-fold** Z-fold wings fold into the centre panel and meet in the middle.

**boxed step** Stock top is cut away horizontally so that each panel decreases in size from the full-size panel. It is then accordion folded.

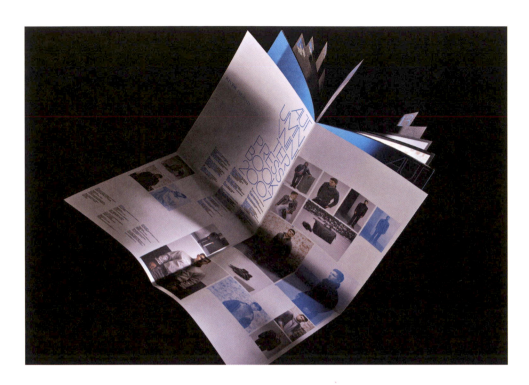

**River Island press book (above)**
The press book of fashion retailer River Island by Third Eye Design features a poster cover that is folded and saddle-stitched to the text block. The poster provides an overview of the book content and also adds a dynamic element to the publication.

**NB: Studio card (below)**
Pictured below is a Christmas card created by and for design studio, NB: Studio, which features a series of box-step folds through which the different panels increase and decrease in size.

**Phaidon mailer (below)**
This mailer/brochure, created by Gavin Ambrose to promote Phaidon's *Art & Ideas* series, features a 16-panel accordion fold. The folds create panels for the logical placement of information while the large number of folds emphasises the breadth of the series it promotes. The front (top) features all the books, current and upcoming in the series, while the reverse (bottom) acts as a frieze, reproducing the covers as a panoramic photograph.

## Land Securities (above)

This brochure was created for Land Securities property development in London's Cheapside by NB: Studio. It features a hardback uncoated board cover that contains a high gloss concertina fold tip-in brochure to provide a contrast of stocks.

## 'Architecture Week' (right)

This edition of architecture magazine, *Architecture Week,* created by designers Nick Hard and Matt Brown, features an A5 brochure **(A)** that folds out **(B)** to reveal a programme guide poster **(C)**. The poster uses parallel and horizontal concertina folds to pack down and form a booklet that can easily be placed into a bag or folder.

**A**

**B**

**C**

## trimming and guillotining

Once a job has been printed, it proceeds to the finishing stage to undergo processes such as trimming, whereby excess stock is cut away from the design to produce the final format. While trimming may fall outside a designer's brief, discussing the trimming requirements with the printer or finishing firm may provide useful information that can be included within the design to avoid finishing problems.

an industrial guillotine

trimmed print work

**NB: Studio Christmas card (above)**
Pictured is a Christmas card created by and for NB: Studio and featuring careful production and trimming to produce this extraordinary Christmas tree effect.

The stock pile bows upwards in the middle as it is securely held.

The cutter blade tends to slide forward as it cuts through a pile of stock.

### cutter draw

A trimming machine has a cutter under which the trim marks a designer has placed on a print job to mark its edges are aligned. The printed pages are held secure and the blade descends under high pressure through the substrate to make the cut.

As there is usually a large number of sheets being cut, a cutter blade has a tendency to slide forward as it passes through the block, as shown in the illustration (bottom left). This may cause bowing in the block of stock (left) as it is securely anchored at either edge. This is more of an issue with lighter stocks.

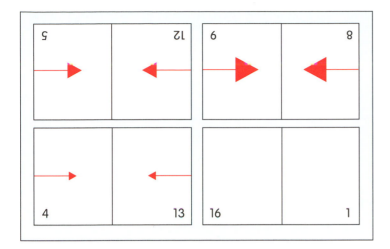

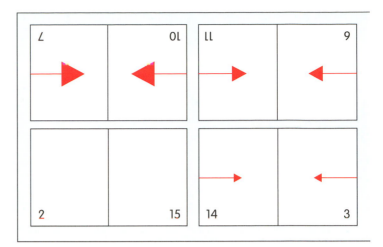

## amending artwork to compensate for creep

Books are typically made of sections of folded pages that nest within each other and are bound together. As such, they can be subject to creep, a process whereby the inner pages extend beyond the outer pages, particularly with thicker stocks. However, a publication can be designed to take account of potential creep problems.

Modern print finishing workshops often feature guillotines that have a computer-controlled system to ensure trim consistency and accuracy to within 1/10 of a millimetre.

High-print-run books and magazines may be trimmed on a three-knife trimmer, a cutting machine that trims all three edges in two cuts. The fore edge knife makes the first cut and then the other two knives simultaneously cut the head and tail.

A guillotine is a single-knife cutter with a heavy blade that descends between vertical runners. A guillotine has a table on which the material to be cut is piled; a movable back gauge or fence, which is perpendicular to the table and against which the back edge of the pile rests; a clamp or press beam that compresses and secures the front edge of the pile that is to be cut; and a cutter. Modern cutters feature automatic spacing that causes the back gauge to move a pre-determined distance following each cut. For safety reasons, controls are designed to require both hands to be used to activate cutting operations.

A simple imposition plan (above) allows a designer to alter the artwork of a publication to allow for creep. Repositioning elements on the pages of a section that are affected most, such as folios, means that they will be in the same place on every printed page. The red arrows in the illustration represent the degree of movement necessary. The bigger the arrow, the more movement needed.

This illustration shows how the nesting of the pages in a section can result in the projection of excess paper at the trim edge.

## over-runs and quantities

Once a job has been printed it is delivered to a client or sent to a print finisher if further finishing processes are required. If the print order was for 1,000 copies you would expect 1,000 to be delivered, but this does not always happen as many copies go to waste while a printing press is being run up, getting the colours correct and so on. If a job is to be sent to a finishing house for spot UV printing, die cutting or foiling, a printer usually prints more copies to allow for the wastage at the finishing house as they set up their equipment.

A printer may print overs – extra copies for your files – depending upon your relationship with the firm, but unless you specifically ask for 1,000 copies as a minimum, you may get fewer delivered as the 1,000 printed copies will be depleted due to the wastage from the various processes. A printer will not restart the press for a missing 50 copies and legally, they do not have to, so the best option is to speak with the printer and be explicit about how many copies are needed.

# glossary

Print production features a wealth of specialist vocabulary to describe different processes, attributes and characteristics. A working knowledge of these terms is essential to ensure accurate communication between design professionals, printers, suppliers and clients.

This glossary is intended to define some of the most commonly used terms, including those that are often confused or used inappropriately. An appreciation and understanding of these terms will facilitate a better understanding and articulation of the print-production process.

**'Dyson' (facing page)**
Pictured is a case-bound book created by design studio Thirteen for vacuum cleaner producer Dyson, which features a debossed title that creates a very subtle cover.

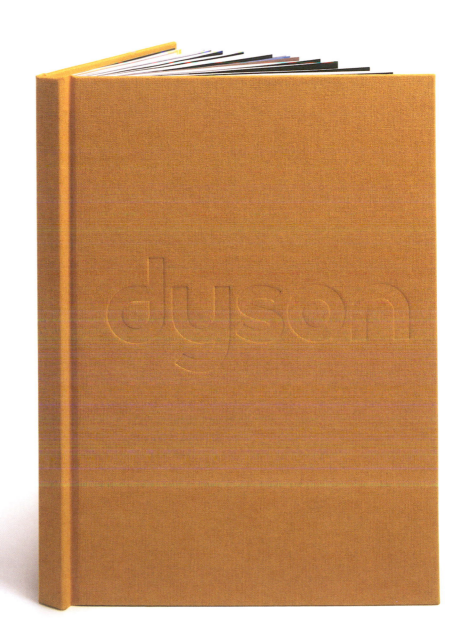

**Absolute measurement**
A finite, fixed value, such as a millimetre.

**Binding**
A process through which the various pages that comprise a printed work are gathered and securely held together to form a publication.

**Bitmap**
A raster image that is composed of pixels in a grid.

**Bounce**
A registration problem occurring when non-colour areas print adjacent to heavy colour areas.

**Bounding box**
The square around a digital image whose anchors can be pulled to distort the image.

**Brightness**
How light or dark a colour is. Also called value.

**Bulk**
The width of a book block.

**Burn**
An image manipulation technique that lightens tones.

**Calliper**
The thickness or bulk of a stock.

**Channels**
The stored colour information of a digital image.

**Clipping paths**
Vector lines used to isolate areas of an image.

**CMYK**
The subtractive primary colours used as process colours in four-colour printing.

**Colour cast**
An imbalance in the colours of an image that leaves one dominant.

**Colour correction**
Techniques to optimise colour performance and remove casts.

**Colour management**
A process governing colour translation through the different stages of the printing process.

**Colour scales**
Graduated reference cards printed with precise colours to ensure accurate colour reproduction when scanning.

**Colour space**
The array of colours that a graphic device can reproduce.

**Curves**
Adjustable graphs used to define an image's colour and tonality.

**Depth of field**
The distance in front of and beyond a subject that is in focus.

**Die cutting**
Use of a steel die to decoratively cut away stock.

**Dodge**
An image manipulation technique that darkens tones.

**Dot gain**
The spreading and enlarging of ink dots on the stock during printing.

**Dpi**
Dots per inch, a measure of print resolution.

**Duotones, tritones and quadtones**
Tonal images produced from a monotone original and the use of two, three or four colour tones.

**Duplexing**
The bonding of two stocks to form a single substrate with different characteristics each side.

**Em**
A relative unit of typographical measurement linked to type size.

**Embossing and debossing**
The use of a steel die to stamp a design into a substrate to produce a decorative raised or indented surface.

**En**
A relative unit of typographical measurement linked to type size that is equal to half an em.

**End pages**
Pages that secure the text block to the boards of the cover in a case binding.

**Flaps**
An extension of a book cover or dust jacket that fold back and into the publication.

**Foil**
A finishing process applying coloured foil to a substrate via a heated die.

**Folding**
Different methods for turning a printed sheet into a more compact form or signature.

**Four-colour black**
The darkest black produced when all four process colours are overprinted on each other.

**Gamut**
Every possible colour that can be produced with a given set of colourants on a particular device, such as RGB and CMYK.

**Gradient**
The increasing weight of one or more colours.

**Greyscale**
A tonal scale of achromatic tones with varying levels of white and black used to convert continuous-tone colour photographs into approximate levels of grey.

**Half-tone**
An image made from half-tone dots, produced by screening a continuous tone image for printing.

**Head and tailbands**
Protective patterned or coloured bands that form part of a book block binding.

**Hue**
The unique characteristic of a colour formed by different wavelengths of light.

**Imposition**
The sequence and position that pages will print before being cut, folded and trimmed.

**Interpolation**
One of several computer processes used to regenerate an image after it has been resized.

**Laminate**
A layer of plastic coating, heat sealed on to a substrate to produce a smooth and impervious finish.

**Laser cutting**
Use of a laser to cut intricate shapes into a stock.

**Layers**
Different levels of a digital image that can be worked on separately.

**Layout**
The management of form and space in a design.

**Line art**
An image with no tonal variation, fill colour or shading that does not require screening for printing.

**Masks**
A graduated layer or filter that is used to blend different images.

**Moiré**
An interference pattern caused by poor half-tone screen alignment.

**Neutral grey**
A colour made from 50 per cent cyan, 40 per cent magenta and 40 per cent yellow that allows designers to accurately see colour balance by providing a neutral contrast.

**Overprinting**
Where one ink overprints another so that they mix to create different colours.

**Paper grain**
The alignment of paper fibres during the manufacturing process.

**Parallax**
A visual effect that makes an object appear displaced when seen from different viewpoints.

**Perforation**
Cuts in a substrate that allow parts to be detached or to create a decorative effect.

**Pica**
An absolute unit of typographical measurement equal to 12pts. There are six picas in an inch.

**Point**
An absolute unit of typographical measurement. There are 72pts in an inch.

**Ppi**
Pixels per inch, a measure of screen resolution.

**Printing**
One of several processes that apply ink or varnish from a plate to a substrate through the application of pressure.

**Proofing**
Various tests used in the print production process to ensure accurate reproduction.

**Raster**
A fixed resolution image composed of pixels in a grid.

**Recto / verso**
The right- and left-hand pages of a spread.

**Registration black**
A black obtained from 100 per cent coverage of the four process colours (cyan, magenta, yellow and black).

**Relative measurement**
A value determined in relation to a key reference.

**Resolution**
The number of pixels contained in a digital image, expressed as dpi, lpi, ppi or spi.

**Reverse out**
Where a design is an unprinted area in a solid block of colour.

**RGB**
The additive primary colours of white light.

**Rich black**
A black that uses a shiner to prevent the bounce registration problem.

**Saturation**
The purity of a colour and the amount of grey it contains. Also called chroma.

**Scanning**
A process through which an image or piece of artwork is converted into an electronic file.

**Shiner**
The underprinting of a process colour to strengthen a black and prevent registration errors.

**Special characters**
Typographical symbols that may be required when use of the normal character set causes problems.

**Stochastic printing**
Use of different dots sizes and random placement to avoid the appearance of moiré patterns.

**Stock**
The substrate that a job is printed upon.

**Text block**
The book block of printed signatures or sections of a publication.

**Thermography**
A print finishing process producing raised lettering by fusing thermographic powder to a design in an oven.

**Tint**
A colour printed at ten per cent increments of a full solid colour created using half-tone dots of different sizes.

**Varnish**
A colourless coating applied to a printed piece to protect and enhance visual appearance.

**Vector**
A resolution-independent and scalable image defined by mathematical formulae or paths rather than pixels.

**Z-bind**
A binding method that holds two blocks in a z-shaped cover.

# conclusion

Before you took possession of it, this publication required the work of many different people performing various processes to turn the ideas presented here into a physical printed product. In this volume we have attempted to explain the key elements of those production processes to provide a better understanding of the steps taken in the design process to obtain the finished product.

The range of different processes involved, from creating the design, selecting paper stocks, and the printing and finishing process are specialist functions that all enjoy their own vocabulary. It is hoped that, with a greater understanding of these techniques, you will be encouraged to try out new and creative print-production methods to create more dynamic and exciting designs.

**Kontroll (above)**

Pictured is a poster created by Research Studios that features the layering of multiple graphic effects over a photograph. This design brings together many of the aspects covered in this book. For example, vector graphics are overlaid over two raster images that have been colour adjusted to produce a pink-red hue. The top layer of the design contains the text, some of which has been reversed out in white, while pink elements knock out of the black background.

# index

# acknowledgements and contacts

We would like to thank everyone who has been involved in the production of this volume, especially all the designers and design studios that generously contributed examples of their work. And a final thank you to Leafy Robinson, Brian Morris and all at AVA Publishing for all their help and support.

All reasonable attempts have been made to clear permissions and credit the copyright holders of the works reproduced in this book. However, if any have been inadvertently omitted, the publisher will endeavour to incorporate amendments in future editions.

| | |
|---|---|
| 3 deep design | www.3deep.com.au |
| Gavin Ambrose | www.gavinambrose.co.uk |
| Faydherbe/De vringer | www.ben-wout.nl |
| NB: Studio | www.nbstudio.co.uk |
| Parent. | www.parentdesign.co.uk |
| Peter and Paul | www.peterandpaul.co.uk |
| Research Studios | www.researchstudios.com |
| Robert Petrie | |
| SEA | www.seadesign.co.uk |
| Social | www.socialuk.com |
| Spin | www.spin.co.uk |
| Studio Output | www.studio-output.com |
| Studio Thomson | www.studiothomson.com |
| Thirteen | www.thirteen.co.uk |
| Third Eye Design | www.thirdeyedesign.co.uk |
| Webb & Webb | www.webbandwebb.co.uk |

**image credits**

image on page 154 (top right) © stephmcg

images on page 155 (right) © The Gentle Group

images on pages 21, 59, 63, 81, 159 (middle), 167, 168, 169 (bottom left), 170 (top left), 171 (top left, bottom left, bottom right), 173 (top left), 174 (left), 175 (top right, bottom left), 176 (right), 177 (right), 180 (right), 191 © Xavier Young <www.xavieryoung.co.uk>